Precious Metal Clay Techniques

CONTEMPORARY TECHNIQUES FROM TEN ARTISTS

....

Edited by Tim McCreight

A & C BLACK • LONDON

tech·nic (tek' nik) n. 1. *Plural*. The theory, principles, or study of an art of process. 2. *Plural*. Technical details, rules, methods, or the like.

First published in Great Britain 2007
A&C Black Publishers Limited
38 Soho Square
London W1D 3HB
www.acblack.com

Copyright 2007 Brynmorgen Press

ISBN 978-0-7136-8757-6

Published in the USA by
Brynmorgen Press
58 Wasington Avenue

Portland, Maine 04101

A CIP catalogue record for this book
is available from the British Library.

Cover designed by James Watson

Printed and bound in Hong Kong by
Elegance Printing Company Ltd

All designs are the property of the artists.

Photo Credits

Davidson	Drew Davidson
Fago	Robert Diamante
Kahn	Robert Diamante
King	Drew Davidson
Kovalcik	Corrin Jacobsen Kovalcik
Meijerink	Noortje Meijerink
Russell	Robert Diamante
Simon	Robert Diamante
Wire	Robert Diamante
Woell	J. Fred Woell

Drawings by Tim McCreight

Contents

INTRODUCTION

We are fortunate in the jewelry world to have hundreds of workshops taught each year. Talented artists take time from their lives to develop not only their technical skills, but their ability to convey their ideas with clarity and enthusiasm. But even those people who happily call themselves Workshop Junkies can't hope to attend all the classes they would like. That's where this book comes in.

Many years ago, I found myself holding a folder filled with handouts from a variety of workshops that had been given by leaders in the metalsmithing field. These were faded, over-copied, coffee-stained sheets, and they were almost priceless. Each page represented uncounted hours of experimentation, the results of which were gathered and explained by gifted teachers. In order to preserve those gems and at the same time give the information wider exposure, I created a book called *Metals Technic.* As I had hoped, the information continues to live on.

At the time, I felt that the formula would lend itself to other areas of crafts, and I considered a collection of articles on blacksmithing, stonesetting, and surface techniques. None of these felt quite right, so I set the idea aside... until recently. It has been just over ten years since Precious Metal Clay became available to artists. There are now thousands of hobbyists, art students, and professional designers working with PMC. Some of these people have developed unique techniques or approaches, and these, like the handout sheets from a previous generation, deserve to be saved and shared.

This is not a project book—no one is encouraging you to duplicate the work you see here. Instead, this is a record of what can happen when curiosity, passion, and talent spill together. In many cases, the authors who have contributed to this book have devoted many hours to experiments, some ending in triumph, and some ending, well, not in triumph... In science, it is standard practice to share results of experiments so that each generation can build on lessons already learned to advance quickly into new territory. That is the goal of this book. The authors join me in saying this: "Take a look at what I've done, and if it appeals to you, or gives you some ideas, explore them, push against them, then share your results with the world."

Put on a Pedestal
Fine silver, 23.5k gold (keum boo application), aquamarine and labradorite briolettes,
pearls, glass, sterling chain, fine silver and 23.5k gold clasp.

Tonya Davidson

Using the PMC Syringe

The PMC Syringe is one of the most essential tools for PMC work and often the last tool considered. Unfortunately, it seems that many PMC artists think of it as a medium rather than a tool; a means to a specific look, rather than a versatile way to achieve many different effects. The first step in taking full advantage of the syringe is to develop confidence in how to use it. I'll cover that, then go on to describe some of the ways I use a syringe in my work. I have taught many people to overcome their mistrust of Syringe PMC, and I'm confident that the necessary skills can be mastered with the right guidance and practice. Once you learn how to use the syringe, I think you'll find that you use it for many projects. It can be used, for instance, to make filigree, to fill seams, to repair, to embellish, to set stones, to cement pieces together, to make bezels, to make cells for cloisonné enamel, and to build dimension.

BACKGROUND

Initially I got interested in the PMC Syringe when I was looking for an alternate way to make bezels. Using rolled out clay always left them too thick, and I didn't like the effort or the result. I discovered that once I became proficient with the syringe, I could make bezels that had the delicacy of those made in traditional metalsmithing. Once I was comfortable with the syringe as a tool, I found that I reached for it more and more, using it for repairs and to attach parts. In my teaching, I find that many PMC artists have not learned to master this important tool, and as a result, they are missing out on some great opportunities. I hope the instructions here demonstrate how much can be done, and how efficient the syringe can be.

Whether it's a tennis racket or a planishing hammer, a new tool requires instruction and practice in how to hold it. In the case of the PMC Syringe, it is important to hold the syringe so you can deliver confident force without strain (and the wiggle that will come with exertion). The magic is in your thumb, which has much more strength than any finger. Lay the syringe across your palm so that the tip pokes out at the heel of your closed fist. People with large hands might find that the tip needs to emerge between their middle finger and ring finger, while curling the pinkie and ring finger into the palm. This makes it possible to see what they are doing without their hand obscuring or touching the work. This position works for most people, but if it doesn't, try holding the syringe with the plunger centered in the middle of your palm, with the tip exiting between the middle and ring finger. This will allow your palm to do most of the work.

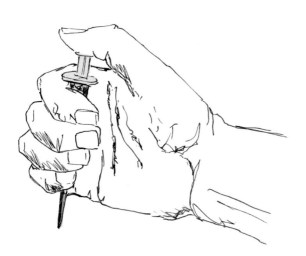

The best way to hold the syringe is across the palm so your thumb can press the plunger.

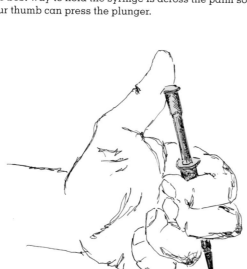

People with large hands might find it better to let the syringe tip poke out between their fingers, like this. For some people, this allows better viewing of the extruded line.

Many people try to control the syringe and execute precision work with shoulder and bicep muscles. Because those muscles are so far distant from the hand, they cannot help much with control. Instead, learn to control your hand like this. Use the index finger of your opposite hand to create a bridge with your index finger (like painters do with their steady stick). Locate the lunate bone at the outside of your palm nearest the wrist. By pressing against this bone on the hand that operates the syringe, you'll find that your non-syringe hand can steer with great control. This allows you to relax your arm and shoulder and concentrate on the task at hand. In situations where the index finger/lunate bone does not offer control, try using the fingertips of your opposite hand to support the side of your syringe.

For maximum control, brace your hand by pressing the index finger of your other hand against the bones of your wrist. If that feels awkward, replace the single index finger with the three fingers of your other hand.

Peaceful Capture
Fine silver, CZ briolettes, pearls, semiprecious stone beads. The filigree grille was made with a 16 gauge ribbon tip.

RELATED TOOLS

Most companies that sell PMC also offer the factory made, preloaded syringe. This version of metal clay is specially formulated to allow it to be forced through a small nozzle. All types of PMC can be thinned with water to allow them to be extruded, but once they leave the nozzle, the diluted clay sags and loses all traces of its original extruded shape. The syringe is ready to use, but to get the most from this versatile tool, I recommend a few additional tools.

The syringe is packaged with a plastic tip that will extrude a round 20 gauge thread (.032" or 0.8 mm). Additional tips that fit onto the syringe are available in a variety of shapes and sizes, including round wires from 14 to 22 gauge (1.6–0.8 mm), flat ribbon tips from 14 through 18 gauge (1.6–1 mm) half-round wires from 14 to 18 gauge (1.6–1 mm), and even a square tip in 16 gauge (1.3 mm). Using the syringe without any tip offers a round rod of approximately 13 gauge (1.83 mm). These designations refer to sizes before firing; final dimensions will be about 15% smaller.

The choice of which tip to use for specific projects depends partly on the visual effect you are seeking, and partly on the strength that is required. Bear in mind that a delicate wire has proportionately less contact with the surface, and risks being torn away in high stress applications. And no matter which tip you use, be sure to pat down beginning and ending portions of extruded lines with a

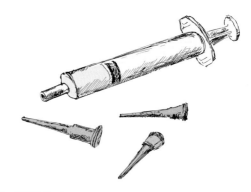

The PMC Syringe comes loaded with a version of metal clay that is specially formulated to extrude. The package includes one tip, and others can be purchased separately. Syringe material can be used with all other versions of PMC.

The upper line in each example is the unfired extruded line, which is roughly the size of the B&S gauge number shown beside it (made with the syringe, of course). The lower line has been fired and is a bit smaller as a result.

The top group uses round syringe tips. The lower six lines are as follows:

14g ribbon

14g half-round

16g ribbon

16 half-round

18g ribbon

18g half-round

damp brush. These are the areas most likely to lift off the surface, so make a habit of insuring that they are well secured to the surface.

To harness the full potential of syringe metal clay, you will want a couple high quality paint brushes. I use a size 0 synthetic brush, to move and model most of my extruded lines. You may prefer a 2/0 or even 3/0 as well. Larger size brushes are more appropriate for brushing on slip. You'll use this brush to move, adjust, pick up, or remove any syringe line that is not desired. Keep in mind that wet clay sticks to wet clay, so proper use of the syringe involves constant monitoring of moisture content. This is more intuitive than cerebral, but it reminds us that you'll have a clean brush in your hand most of the time. A clean brush that is slightly damp is one of my favorite and frequently used tools.

To keep syringes from drying out during work sessions, I use a small jar or drinking glass half full of water. The tip should be totally submerged, but there is no reason to have the handle always wet—this just makes it messy to handle. For longer storage between sessions, I press each syringe into a florist's "bud tube." These keep the syringe moist for up to two weeks. For longer storage, put the syringe in a tightly sealed bag with a moistened bit of paper towel.

SYRINGE BASICS

To start a line, touch the tip of the syringe to the surface and depress the plunger. If the clay does not stick to the base where you want it to, dampen the area with a brush, wait a few seconds for the water to soften the PMC, and try again. If the clay coming out of the syringe is not fresh, this will also make it difficult for the new line to adhere. Squeeze out a tiny amount of clay to clear the tip of the nozzle, and try again. Scraps can be put back into your paste jar. To end a syringe line, lower the syringe to the surface and stop depressing the plunger. Touch the surface with the tip of the syringe, and the line will disconnect.

In practice, the syringe should float a few millimeters above the surface, laying a line gracefully onto the surface. If you hold the syringe too high, you sacrifice control over the location of the line. If you hold it too low, there is a risk of bumping the tip into the line, leaving a mark. The pace at which the syringe travels should match the rate at which the clay is being pushed out of the tube. If you travel too slowly, the thread will double back on itself. If you travel too fast, the thread is stretched, and can sometimes break. Neither of these problems is serious, but both under-

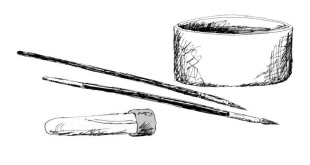

To get the most out of the syringe, you'll want a couple high quality Taklon brushes. To keep an opened syringe from drying out between uses, push it into a florists' water tube.

The syringe should hover about a quarter of an inch above the work, allowing the thread to drop down into position. Touch the tip to the work to start and to terminate a line.

mine your control. Learn to match these two elements—pressing the plunger and steering the thread—and you have mastered Syringe 101.

Most often we see syringe used as embellishment just as it comes from the tube. The range of tips allows for wires that are other than round, but even these do not exhaust the possibilities. You can embellish syringe lines by texturing them when they are semi-hard. Wait a few minutes after extruding, then press the line with a stylus to create lines that appear braided, twisted, or ornamented in other ways. You can also let a syringe line dry, then sand across the top to create the effect of a hammered wire. To achieve an irregular "hammered" effect, flatten a partially dry line with a dampened finger in certain areas.

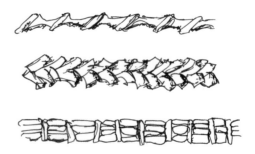

We sometimes forget that a line made with a syringe might be a starting point for further work. Simple tools can alter a syringe line to create striking textures.

Square Peg
Fine silver, 22k gold, pearls, sterling chain, garnet, glass. The syringe was only used to embellish the bail.

USING THE SYRINGE TO BUILD DIMENSION

Build dimension and depth by placing one syringe line on top of a previously dried syringe line. This is a great way to build a bezel or to make cloisonné cells. In most cases, I start with the broad round line that comes from the syringe itself. Remove the tip, dampen the surface lightly to insure a good bond, and squeeze out a broad line in the shape desired. Refine the line with a damp brush, lifting, sliding, or otherwise adjusting it to create the shape you want. If you are making a closed form, use the damp brush to sculpt the ends together. You may need to add a bit of slip at this time to fill in gaps. Also, if you find that the line was uneven because of stretching, apply slip to build up those areas. This first line is a foundation, so it pays to get it right.

Dry this first layer, then add a second layer of syringe directly on top of the first layer, again using the untipped syringe. Mend and adjust with a damp brush as needed, then allow the second layer to dry thoroughly. To develop a delicate wall (like a bezel, for instance), make a third layer with the 18 gauge (pink) tip, centered on the ridge that you've

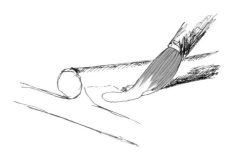

Paint slip along the base of a syringe thread to merge it into the surface. This has the double effect of added strength and visual harmony.

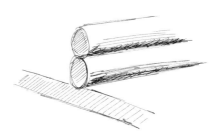

To build a bezel, lay down a single syringe line, allow it to dry, then lay another on top of the first.

She's the Bee's Knees
Fine silver, resin
The syringe was used for ornamentation on the front and back.
4" high

Fine silver band, 22k and 24k gold, raw diamonds. Silver syringe was used to do the swirl in silver and 22k syringe was used for the base of the gold ring around the bottom to mimic the texture of the top.

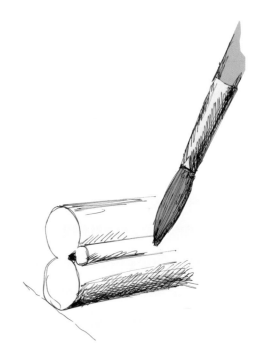

To fill the space between the two structural lines, slide a small tip onto the syringe and extrude a line into the space between the two threads.

created. Extrude about a half inch, then stop to pat down the line with a wet brush. This will blend the layers together so the resulting wall doesn't look banded. Continue on, laying down another half inch or so, and smoothing that portion as you go. When you have completed the intended shape, set the work aside and allow it to dry (or speed dry in a dehydrator).

To further perfect and even out the wall in preparation for sanding, I apply PMC slip using a painting technique called "puddle and pull." Dilute slip to the thickness of yogurt, mixing well to make a smooth consistency. Gather a droplet of slip (puddle) on the tip of a brush and touch it against the wall. Lift the brush slightly, allowing the slip to trail behind in a thin thread, and steer this so it lays into the low spots of the bezel wall. Note that you are not brushing or stroking the slip, but grabbing a thread of slip gathered by surface tension and pulling it across the area you want to fill. Once you get the hang of it, this method is faster than applying several layers of slip, and creates a denser result.

When the slip is completely dry, sand the sides with sanding sticks or miniature files to create a perfect bezel. For me, this method of building a bezel is quicker than using clay and allows me the freedom to work with free-form shapes.

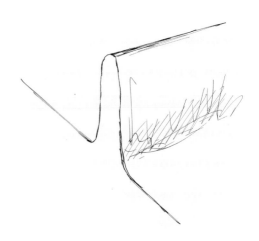

When the bezel wall has dried, lay thick slip along the wall to create an even surface. Smooth with a damp brush as needed, dry, then sand.

MAKING FILIGREE BEADS

The PMC Syringe lends itself to making hollow filigree beads. I like to use cork clay as a core, but almost any combustible material will work. The goal is to have a core that is easily formed, and that will burn away safely midway through the firing process. If using cork, be sure it is thoroughly dry before applying PMC—a process that can take 24 hours naturally or as little as two hours in a dehydrator.

A filigree bead offers an excellent demonstration of just how PMC shrinks, and why it is important to understand the phenomenon. Metal clay shrinks; the spaces between parts, which are made of "air" do not. Imagine a bead made up of small PMC rings. In our minds' eye, the whole bead shrinks, pulling all the parts together. In reality, each metal ring shrinks, pulling in on itself and away from the adjacent rings, which are, of course, drawing in on themselves too. Understanding this effect, we can see why it is important to secure the bonds between each component. Use a brush well-loaded with slip to reinforce each joint. As each unit shrinks, this will hold them together and force them to remain bonded.

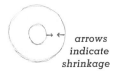

arrows indicate shrinkage

This drawing shows how shrinkage will affect a PMC ring. The silver parts will shrink, but the center hole will not—it is made of air, which doesn't shrink. The ring will be smaller after firing than it was before, but the hole will be about the same.

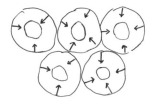

This means there is a tendency to pull apart; reinforce joints to protect against this.

Agua Dulce
Fine silver, limoge painted enamels, pearls, chalcedony, glass, sterling beads. The syringe was used in the back to join the inner piece to the outer square frame.

Start by marking the location of the bead holes with a Sharpie. Make sure to engineer the holes so the bead doesn't tilt forward or hang lopsided. With a syringe, make a circle on that spot, remembering that the holes should be large enough so that even after shrinking, a cord can fit through easily. Allow the ring to dry, then add a second layer on top of this first line, just as described for a bezel. In this case there is no need to hide the lines between the rings because other embellishments on the bead will cover them up.

Once the bead rings are in place, extrude lines on the cork that are well connected to these cord holes. Extrude a line, then confirm the bond to the ring by patting the joint with a wet brush. The possibilities for pattern development are huge, and include layering lines of different sizes, using symmetrical or asymmetrical lines, or adding dots and other pieces. Avoid gaps and large open spaces because they can create weak areas.

USING SYRINGE ON GLASS

When applying PMC to glass, the idea is to achieve a temperature at which the glass is soft enough to fuse with the silver, but not so soft that the silver sinks into it or it begins to enter full fuse stages. At high temperatures, the silver might cause discoloration, and introduce risks associated with the different expansion/contraction rates of metal and glass. I recommend firing all soda lime glass (this includes dichroic Bullseye, Moretti, Spectrum, etc.) with PMC at 1200° F (650° C) for 35 minutes. Pyrex and borosilicate glass require more advanced techniques and hotter temperatures. Because these colors change with the application of heat due to crystallization there are other methods that one must take for success. As this would imply, it is important to know what kind of glass has been used to make a bead you want to embellish with PMC. If you don't know, you can experiment, but understand that there is a risk of discoloration and bonding issues.

Make sure the bead is free of dust and oil, and extrude PMC from the syringe onto the glass just as described above. It is also possible to ornament a glass bead with slip or thin sheets of PMC, but remember not to enclose the bead so much that shrinkage will

Make a core from a combustible material such as paper clay, cork clay, or Styrofoam. Start by marking the location of the holes with a marker.

Extrude a ring of PMC around the mark. Allow it to dry, then flow another ring on top of the first. Depending on the design, these rings can be refined or not.

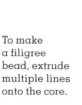

To make a filigree bead, extrude multiple lines onto the core.

put stress on the glass. Allow the embellishment to dry, then clean away haze or dust from the unwanted clay by using a pointed makeup applicator (or similar tool) with glass cleaner or alcohol.

Again, the schedule I recommend as a good place to start is a hold time of 35 minutes at 1200° F (650° C). If the glass slumps, lower the temperature to 1175° F (635° C) on the next firing. Remember that glass is susceptible to thermal shock in both the heating and cooling stages. The larger the bead, the more important it is to heat and cool slowly. Especially for larger beads, ramp up slowly, between 250 and 1500 degrees Fahrenheit per hour. Especially for large beads, I recommend soaking the bead at the annealing temperature of 940°–960° F (about 510° C) for 20 minutes to an hour. The general rule is 15 minutes per quarter-inch of thickness. After that, allow the bead to cool to room temperature before opening the kiln. It is tempting to peek into the kiln during the annealing process, but don't do it!

Glass workers will be sensitive to a problem called devitrification. This refers to the possible creation of a thick, semi-opaque film that can form on glass as it cools. The solution for this, called crash cooling, is not necessary in this case because this method (which uses PMC3) does not go above 1300° F (700° C). Similarly, concerns about yellowing are avoided at these temperatures, because the silver is not heated to temperatures at which fuming occurs. One other potential problem, cracking, is avoided by staying below the temperatures at which the glass becomes viscous. At those high temperatures, the glass is expanding just as the metal clay is shrinking, so stresses are inevitable. Full sintering of PMC3 takes place at safe temperatures that avoid this problem.

To add PMC elements along with syringe lines, I recommend pre-firing the PMC shapes either with a torch or kiln. I usually use PMC Paper, either one or two thickness, but you could use thin sheets of PMC clay also. Hold the fired shape in tweezers and apply some slip or syringe to the backside. Flip this over and lay the pasted shape onto the glass, working quickly enough that the slip remains gooey. Because the sheet is so thin, even when laminated with two layers, it can easily conform to the shape below. When the slip is dry, clean up smudges and remove unwanted clay dust from the glass surface. If you do not pre-fire the shapes, you risk two things happening. First, you may get a hazing around the shape as it shrinks on the surface, making it less pristine. Second, putting slip on a small floppy sheet shape is challenging and can be frustrating.

Azul Tapestry
Fine silver, 22k and 24k gold, sapphire, sterling chain. The syringe was used to set the stone, set the 24k granules, to do the caging in 22k on the sides of the stone and the back of the piece.

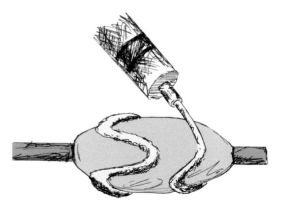

Syringe PMC can be applied to glass, for instance a bead like this. If you don't know the melting point of the glass, you should experiment to be sure it is compatible with PMC. If possible, use wavy threads, which will allow for shrinkage.

Using syringe on ceramic

Syringe PMC can be applied to glazed ceramic objects, using the application methods described above. As with glass, allow the syringe clay to dry, then refine by filing, if necessary, and clean away any excess with a fine brush and glass cleaner.

Firing on ceramic is almost the reverse of the instructions just given for glass. In this case, we want a quick firing that gets as hot as the PMC will allow—1650° F (900° C) for 10 minutes. This will ensure a solid bond between the metal and glaze. Glazes contain a form of ground glass called frit, and those with less frit (matte glazes, for example), are less reliable in creating fusion. Raku glazes contain copper, and this makes the surface especially soft when the glaze melts. For this reason, use only thicker elements on raku glaze. Thin pieces will sink below the surface of the glaze, which is not desirable.

Glazed beads must be placed on stilts or hung from rods during firing, to prevent the glaze from sticking to the kiln shelf. An object with an unglazed underside can be placed directly on a fiberboard shelf, but I recommend reserving shelves just for this use to prevent silver stain contamination onto glass from shelf cross use.

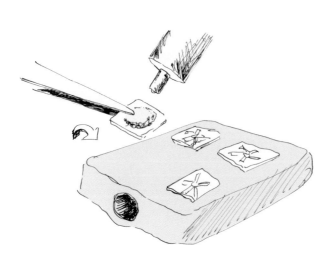

To apply ornamental elements, pre-fire them, then place a dab of syringe on the back of each piece and press it onto the glass. Fire at 1200° F (650° C).

Fire glass or ceramic beads on a rack or stilt of some kind. These are commercially available, or you can use a piece of nichrome wire suspended between a couple pieces of soldering board or posts.

Setting stones with PMC syringe

Another fantastic use for the syringe is to use it to make bezels for stonesetting. With practice, you'll be able to make fast and clean settings. Let me describe the process I use to make a bezel for a round faceted stone as a way to demonstrate this technique.

First, using a craft knife that you have dipped in water, begin to turn the blade while holding it perpendicular to the clay. The water acts as a lubricant, allowing the hole to be drilled smoothly. The sharp point on the blade makes a conical hole that will accommodate the underside of the stone. Clean out the hole with a brush, then use a syringe to build up the bezel. Extrude three or four circles, one upon the other, as if you were creating the levels of a parking garage. These lines should lie at the outer shape of your stone, centered over the hole. The number of layers will depend on the size of your stone—very small stones may only require two rings, while a larger stone may require as many as six.

Next, use a damp brush to shape and clean up the extruded lines. Wet clay sticks to wet clay, so if your brush becomes loaded with clay, it is difficult to control. To prevent this, clean your brush frequently by dipping it in water and shaking off the excess periodically. With a little practice you'll find that you can push, pull, pat, and generally manipulate the syringe line to match the shape of the stone.

When the bezel is prepared, pick up the stone in tweezers and drop it into place. When you have it centered and straight, hold the closed tweezers straight up from the stone. Push down until the clay oozes up over the girdle of the stone, so that when the PMC shrinks it will not expose the girdle. Allow the setting to dry, then check it carefully for traces of PMC on the stone. Remove these with a fine point and a bit of water or glass cleaner. If allowed to fire there, the tiny silver specks will look like flaws in the gem. This is also the time to refine the bezel by light sanding if it has become distorted. Small narrow sanding sticks are great for this, as well as nail files and jewelry files. Once you master this method, I think you'll find that with less work you are creating bezels that are more precise.

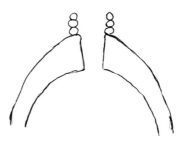

Use a dampened blade to cut a hole for a gemstone. By rotating this style of X-Acto blade, you'll quickly make a neat, conical opening.

Repairing with syringe

The syringe also has many uses for repair work and for joins. Often we reach for slip but this version of PMC has more air and water than other types of PMC, and that makes it less desirable for repairs and joins. I use the syringe to extrude soft, dense PMC onto voids, cracks, and nicks, then pat the material down with a damp brush. The process is quick and the results are usually better than using slip, which often leaves tiny air pockets. Problems with slip are particularly frustrating because the pinholes often don't appear until you begin to sand the top layer.

Triangular Box
Fine silver, Aura 22, 24k gold keum-boo, yellow brass.
2" tall by 1³⁄₈" wide.

Celie Fago

PMC Hinges

uring the past several years, I have tried many approaches to making hinges in PMC, and many different types of hinges. Engineering a hinge on a jewelry scale is an exacting endeavor. An excellent way to understand what makes hinges work, or not work, is to look at hinges: on your door, your car, in your medicine cabinet, your kitchen, and in your jewelry box. Precision is an integral part of hinges, but precision is not what first comes to mind when thinking about PMC. This only serves to make it a more enticing challenge.

In my early boxes and lockets, I made hinges by wrapping fresh PMC+ around a metal mandrel. When the clay dried, I cut the tube into sections (called knuckles) and connected them to the body of the piece. Although the hinges functioned well, wrapping PMC+ around a tiny needle or brass rod is tedious and virtually impossible to do on a very small scale. As a result, my firs t hinges were larger than I wanted them to be. PMC Paper wrapped around a mandrel also worked as a hinge but yielded a delicate result, which limited its use. Also, because the PMC Paper is a flexible material and difficult to stiffen, cutting a tube made from PMC Paper into knuckles is difficult.

My next direction was to use fine silver wire wrapped into a tight coil around a mandrel. I cut this tube-like structure into sections for knuckles and attached them with slip to a PMC box. After firing, it was necessary to file off some of the middle knuckle because, although the box had shrunk, the coils of wire had not. That system worked well enough, but it wasn't ideal. Besides, I wanted to make a hinged box entirely out of PMC.

Hinges made of fine silver tubing, cut into knuckles and attached to a PMC box have the same result as the coiled fine silver wire: adjustments had to be made because the box had shrunk and the silver had not. Alongside this problem, I found that fine silver tubing is difficult to find commercially. Hinges made from sterling tube become brittle when held at high temperatures for the length of time needed to fuse them securely, so firing sterling hinges in place is not an option either.

Clay extruders, made for PMC, have adaptors that allow you to extrude fresh PMC tubing. As extruded, the tubing is too large for most of my hinge applications. However if you dry the extruded tube straight and cut it into short lengths, it can be reduced using the turning method described later in this chapter. Once the tube is reduced, the inside hole can be bored out by drilling, giving you control over the inside and the outside diameter. The advantage of this tool over hand making your tube from scratch is that extruded tube has a straight shaft through it at the start. This is no small advantage.

That brought me to using traditional soldering methods to attach sterling hinges to a PMC object after firing, and while this is possible, part of the point of my developing a viable hinge-making option in PMC was so I could teach it to non-metalsmiths.

MAKING THE ROD

The first step is to create a rod of PMC that is uniform, symmetrical, and dense. Either PMC+ or PMC3 can be used. I like to work on glass but any smooth clean surface will work as long as it's secure and free of oil. If the work surface moves, tape it down or set it onto non-skid material.

I regularly use reconstituted clay in my work, but not for this process. It is critical that the tubes being made are pristine, so for this purpose I use only PMC fresh out of the package. Pull off a piece the size of a small pea and roll it back and forth on your work surface a few times with your fingers to shape it into a rod. Continue rolling with a rolling rectangle (a clear piece of acrylic sheet cut to convenient size) until it has a uniform diameter. In my experience, a three millimeter rod (about the size of a large wooden match) shrinks to a size appropriate for a one-inch box. It is also a convenient size for experimentation. I find it most efficient to make two or three rods while I'm at it. Each hinge requires only a short length, but the tube needs to be perfect. Having some extra allows me to discard sections that aren't quite right. If you notice cracking as you roll, chalk that roll up to experience, and start over with fresh clay.

Start with fresh clay and roll out a smooth rod. I work on a sheet of glass and use a rectangle of acrylic sheet as a roller. The smooth surface, transparency, and rigidness all combine to make an effective tool.

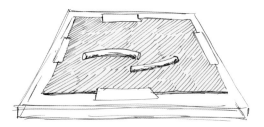

Lay the rods on a piece of Teflon sheet attached to a flat surface and monitor for about a half hour as they dry. Turn them periodically, rolling lightly to counteract warping. If they become curved like these, remoisten and roll again until they are prefectly straight.

It is essential that your hinge rods dry without warping. Set the rods aside where you can monitor drying; every couple of minutes, gently roll the rods a couple of inches back and forth with the rolling rectangle. A piece of Teflon taped to your work surface makes a good place to dry the rods. The action of rolling back and forth between the flat of the desk and the flat of the rolling rectangle keeps the rods straight as they dry. The drying time will vary depending on where you live and the time of year. I usually plan on minding the rods for about half an hour.

Fine silver, gold foil, 18k gold
1½ inches square, ¼ inch deep

TRUING THE RODS BY TURNING

To make the rods precisely round, use a flex
shaft or power drill as a makeshift lathe.
Slide the dry rod into the chuck and tighten
it firmly. If the rod wobbles eccentrically, this
means it is not straight. Small irregularities
will come out in the turning process, but a
major wobble is a signal to stop this process.
Either discard the rod, or undo the warp by
liberally dampening the rod, waiting about
a minute until all evidence of moisture has
disappeared into the surface of the clay. Roll
the rod again on a flat surface, and monitor
the drying process as described previously.

Clamp the dried PMC rod
in a flex shaft or drill press
and rotate it against a
sanding stick that is held
carefully parallel to the
rod. The goal is to make
the rod perfectly round,
smooth, and uniform .

Working over a piece of paper to catch
PMC dust, hold a sanding stick against the
rod while turning the motor at a slow speed. It
is important to have an even pressure against
the rod. Pinch the rod lightly between the
sanding stick and your thumb. As the rod
spins, gently move the sanding stick up and
down the rod to achieve a uniform dimension.
Move from coarse to fine abrasives as needed
to create a uniform, featureless rod. I usually

start with a fine grit Salon Board, then switch to a small piece of 600, then 1000 grit sandpaper. As a last touch, I turn the sandpaper over and hold it against the spinning rod to create a polished surface.

When one half of the rod is uniform and smooth, flip it and refine the other end in the same way. This should yield a piece long enough to cut into two separate hinge tubes, each 20 millimeters long. Set the rods aside, ready when you need them. A good hinge is made to fit a specific object, so you should wait until the piece is complete to determine the length of the hinge and the size of each knuckle.

Measure the hinge area and determine the length of each knuckle. Hinges require at least three knuckles to work well, and look best with an odd number of units, so most hinges use three, five, or seven knuckles. In larger hinges, the knuckles are the same length, but in some cases, such as a small box, the center knuckle (attached to the lid) might be a little longer than the other two. If, for instance, the hinge section measures 15 millimeters across, it would be typical to use three knuckles of four, four, and seven millimeters.

Measure the hinge area and determine what size each knuckle will be. Before drilling, cut the rod into short pieces that will become the knuckles of the hinge.

Locket Pendant with Swing Hinge
Fine silver, polymer clay,
23.5k gold leaf, sterling,
paint pigments
2¾" by 1½" wide

The next step is to drill a shaft down the center of the rod—a critical step that requires great accuracy. It is easier to work on small pieces than to drill the entire rod at once, so now is a good time to talk about cutting this solid rod into the pieces that will eventually be the hinge knuckles. People who anticipate making a lot of hinges will want to invest in a tube cutting jig. This is a heavy metal bar about four inches long that has a V-groove down the center. Both ends are perfectly square, and at one end, two pieces of hardened steel guide a sawblade to keep it running true. A moveable fence makes it easy to cut multiple pieces exactly the same size. These tools are available through jewelry supply companies.

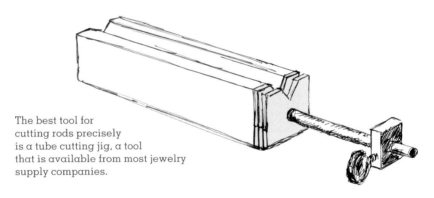

The best tool for cutting rods precisely is a tube cutting jig, a tool that is available from most jewelry supply companies.

Carved Bracelet
Polymer clay, fine silver, sterling, yellow brass

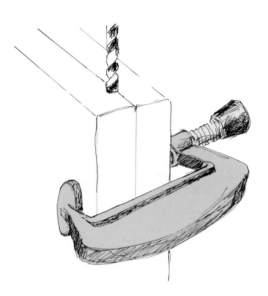

If this is outside your needs at the moment, you can make a useful jig by drilling into a block of hardwood. Clamp two pieces together, and drill several holes of different sizes, making sure that the bit is centered on the interface of the two pieces. It is also critical that the bit be exactly at a right angle to the block. This is relatively easy with a drill press, but can be accomplished with a hand drill and a try square.

Cut the rod into pieces that are a little longer than the final requirement. This will allow for truing up the ends, which can be done by sanding against the end of the tube cutting jig. Cut the rod with a jewelers saw or a tissue blade.

To make an inexpensive alternate to the tube cutting jig, clamp two pieces of wood together and drill a hole so that it spans the two pieces. When they are separated, you will be left with a smooth rounded groove. You might want to drill holes of several sizes to accommodate different rods.

Use a try square to provide visual guidance so the drill is perpendicular to the wood.

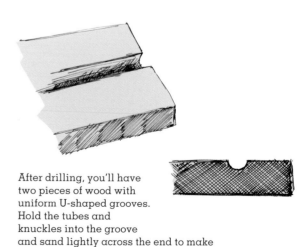

After drilling, you'll have two pieces of wood with uniform U-shaped grooves. Hold the tubes and knuckles into the groove and sand lightly across the end to make perfectly square corners.

DRILLING THE ROD

This delicate step is where your hinge will rise or fall. What is happening is quite simple—you want to drill a hole through the center of the rod, turning it into a tube. Done right, the process will take less time than it takes to read this paragraph. But, like so many things that appear simple, there is more to it than meets the eye. You need to mark the exact center of the rod, start the hole in the right place, drill precisely on the axis of the tube, and end up with a hole that is precisely the correct size. See, nothing to it!

Mark the center of the tube either with the help of a plastic template, or by drawing crosshairs by eye with a sharp pencil. Use a needle to make a tiny indentation exactly in the center. This will help the drill bit find its starting point. To keep the drilling process delicate, I will use at least three "steps" to end up at the intended size hole. I'll start with a very fine drill bit, perhaps on the order of a half millimeter (#70, 22 gauge). I'll follow this with a larger drill bit, and so on until I reach the intended size. With experience, you will find that you can make larger steps, but the first few times, err on the side of caution. Here are two ways to drill the hole that work for me.

When the end of the rod is true and flat, mark the center with a template or center finder. Press a needle into the center to make a tiny dimple.

Bird Box Ring
Fine silver, 24k gold keum-boo, 18k gold, sterling
Box component measures ¾ diameter

USING THE DRILL PRESS

Clamp a small bit into a drill press (or a flex shaft held in a press stand), and rotate the chuck to be sure it is properly centered. For safety's sake, tie back long hair and tuck in loose clothing that might get caught in the drill press as it spins. You will be leaning in close, so this bit of advice is even more important than usual. Position the drill press table so when you hold the rod against the table, the tip of the bit is almost touching. You need to be comfortable and properly braced to have control, so use a chair or stool if you can.

Turn on the drill press, running at a slow speed, and slide the rod upward onto the spinning bit. When the bit is halfway into the rod, let go and allow the tube to rotate. If you are straight and centered, the rod will rotate smoothly; almost invisibly. If the rod makes an eccentric, wobbly arc, you know you have missed the center and that you are coming through at an angle. Pull the rod off and try again from the other end. When the first hole is complete in all knuckle sections, move to a larger bit and repeat the process. Tubing with a hole made by a #56 bit will use an 18 gauge hinge pin after the hinge is fired.

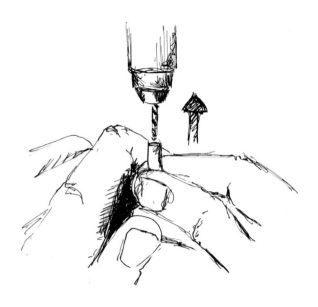

When using a drill press, hold the rod in your fingers, steady both hands, then slowly lift the rod upwards into the rotating bit.

This close-up view shows the precision of a well-made hinge. Note also the bolster that provides extra thickness and strength for the hinge area—and in this case also provides additional ornamentation.

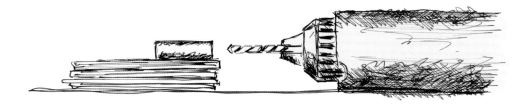

USING A FLEX SHAFT

If you don't have a drill press to keep the bit traveling vertically, here is a way to use a flex shaft to drill a true horizontal. As before, make a rod, dry it well, make it uniform, cut it into sections, true the ends, and mark the center point. Put the fine drill bit into the flex shaft and position the handpiece on a smooth hard surface such as the top of a workbench. Use pieces of wood, plastic, and metal to build a platform that will bring the rod to the precise height at which the drill bit matches the center point. It might be necessary to use shims like playing cards) to fine tune the height. Lower yourself so the stack is at eye level to see the situation clearly. When the stack is properly made, you can turn your attention to running the bit straight into the rod. For this, I stand above the rod so I can sight down on it from directly above.

When using a flex shaft, raise the tube on a stack of cards (or any other collection of materials) so that the center point exactly matches the height of the drill bit when the handpiece is flat on the workbench. Stand over the work, looking straight down, while drilling to be sure you run straight through the center of the rod.

Locket Pendant
Fine silver, paper, polymer clay, sterling

PREPARATION FOR THE HINGE

Now that the knuckles are ready to go, it is time to prepare the area that will receive the hinge. This could be links of a bracelet, a lidded box, or segments of a neckpiece. Each design will present unique challenges, but the following comments apply to most situations.

There is no "close enough" in hinges. Be exacting; if something is out of line, fix it. If parts don't fit precisely, refine them with sandpaper or a blade until they match perfectly. Don't put off these adjustments until later. No matter how awkward they seem now, they will be more difficult after firing. Deal with them.

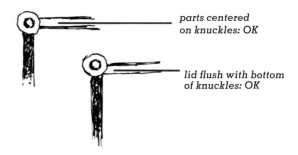

parts centered on knuckles: OK

lid flush with bottom of knuckles: OK

It is important to consider the location of the hinge knuckles to insure a hinge that works smoothly. Be sure the parts (for instance, the lid and walls of a box) do not impinge on one another.

1. Hinges can line up in several ways and still operate, but there are a few configurations that just won't work. One of the advantages of building a hinge in PMC is that we can test this before completing the hinge. Still, it makes sense to plan ahead to avoid arrangements that just won't work.

In both these examples, the lid will press against the box and be unable to open.

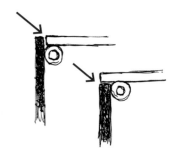

2. Hinges often take a lot of stress, so it is typical to reinforce the area around the hinge. In addition to providing more strength, a bolster gives more contact for the hinge, which makes the union of tube to box (or whatever) stronger too.

The reinforcing piece can be on the inside like this or on the outside.

In some cases, it is a good idea to reinforce the area that will hold the hinge. In this box, for example, the top of the back wall is made thicker by adding a piece of PMC.

SETTING THE KNUCKLES

In most cases, the PMC object (box, bracelet, etc.) will be almost completely finished before attaching the hinge. For illustration purposes, I'll show a hinge on a bracelet. The first step in assembly is to measure the total length of the hinge, then cut knuckles to size. In this example, I'll divide the length by three, and cut tube lengths with a jewelers saw. As stated before, it is important that the ends of all knuckles are at a right angle to the hole.

Slide the knuckles onto a piece of straightened wire that fits tightly through the hole. This will keep them in alignment. Set the parts in their final position, for instance by putting a lid on a box, or, in this case, laying the panels end to end. Set the hinge into place, and look carefully at the area where the knuckles touch the panels. The better this fit, the stronger the final hinge will be. If the fit is poor, lift the tubing away and sand or carve the area.

Use thick slip to cement the center knuckle to the panel. It is very important to use thick slip for this step. Not only is thick slip stronger than thin slip (more material, less water), but it will dry without seeping into places where you don't want it to go. Make this initial connection with just enough slip to hold the knuckle in position. Later you'll beef up the joint. Set it aside to dry, knuckle side up. When the center knuckle is dry, check alignment with the other knuckles. If everything lines up properly, use thick slip to secure the outer knuckles. As with the center knuckle, use just enough slip to tack the elements in place. Again, set aside to dry completely.

When the initial tack joints are dry, reinforce the attachment of knuckles to panels by pressing a small rod of PMC into the joint. Dampen the space with water, then use a brush or a rubber tip to press the PMC firmly into the space between the knuckle and the object. This provides strength and also makes the hinge integrate visually into the piece. Do this on all the knuckles, top and bottom. Set aside to dry; resist the temptation to abbreviate this step. Let it get really, really dry.

To test the hinge, slide a wire through it and gently open it. Sand any sticking points carefully with a small folded strip of sandpaper, rechecking frequently so you don't go too far and create gaps between the knuckles. The hinge should function at this stage.

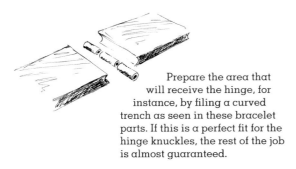

Prepare the area that will receive the hinge, for instance, by filing a curved trench as seen in these bracelet parts. If this is a perfect fit for the hinge knuckles, the rest of the job is almost guaranteed.

Slide a temporary hinge pin through the tubes to hold them in alignment.

Attach the center knuckle with thick slip. When dry, check the alignment with the other two. If they line up correctly, attach the outer knuckles. Dry completely then test the hinge to be sure it works. Remove the pin, separate the parts, and reinforce the joints as needed.

REPAIRING ALIGNMENT

If the hinge operates stiffly, it could be because the knuckles do not line up. To fix this, dampen the out-of-line knuckle by wetting the joint well with a brush. Let the water seep into the joint at the point where the crooked knuckle connects. Give the water a minute to be absorbed into the joint, then slide a tight-fitting wire into the knuckle and gently lever it into place. If it won't move, wick more water into the joint, front and back, wait until it is absorbed, then try again. When you can move it, realign it with the other knuckles, and press it firmly into place. Allow the piece to dry, then reinforce this knuckle with thick slip.

FIRING

Separate the parts and fire them at 1650° F (900° C). PMC+ and PMC3 can be fired for as short a time as ten minutes but I always fire at 1650° F for 30–60 minutes. If the knuckles moved slightly out of alignment during firing, you can nudge them back with your fingers, a scribe, or a tight mandrel, using gentle pressure. If you use pliers, first slide a tight-fitting mandrel into the knuckle you are trying to realign.

Fire the parts separately.

Triangular Box
Fine silver, Aura 22, 24k gold keum-boo, yellow brass
2" high by 1³/₈" wide

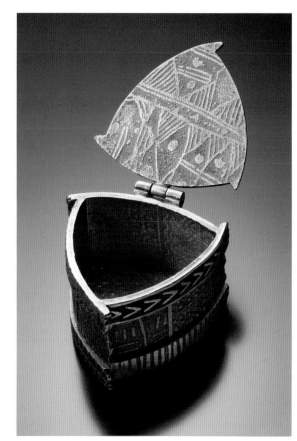

Can I make the knuckles different sizes?
Hinges usually consist of an uneven number of knuckles, and they are typically the same size. In boxes with three knuckles, it is not uncommon to make the center knuckle longer than the other two.

Can I put a hinge on a curved surface?
Yes, but the hinge itself must not be curved. Prepare the parts by filing a straight groove that will cradle the hinge. Examples of this can be found on pocket watches, compacts, and round pill boxes.

NO. This arrangement won't open.

YES. The hinge itself is straight.

Hinges can be applied to a curved form like a round box, but the hinge itself needs to be straight. This is usually accomplished by filing into the curve or adding a flange.

What special tools are helpful for hingemaking?
I mentioned the tube cutting jig earlier. In addition to that, a small try square is helpful. They are available through hobby shops that specialize in model railroading, and as an alternative, I use a sliding brass millimeter gauge. Separate the pieces and you'll find you have two useful squares. I couldn't get along without my jewelers saw; if you haven't bought and mastered that, I'd put it on your list. I also rely on needle files, and their smaller sibling, called escapement files.

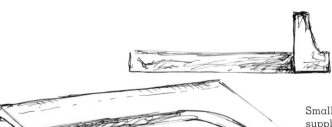

Small squares are available from jewelry supply houses, and you can also use the parts of a sliding millimeter gauge.

Jennifer Kahn

PMC Bezels

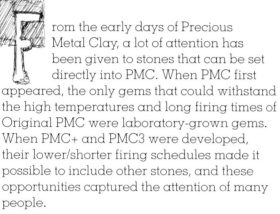rom the early days of Precious
Metal Clay, a lot of attention has
been given to stones that can be set
directly into PMC. When PMC first
appeared, the only gems that could withstand
the high temperatures and long firing times of
Original PMC were laboratory-grown gems.
When PMC+ and PMC3 were developed,
their lower/shorter firing schedules made it
possible to include other stones, and these
opportunities captured the attention of many
people.

Still, there are hundreds of gem materials
that cannot be set until after firing is complete. Articles and books describe how to use
calibrated sizes for which commercial settings
are available, and while this extends possibilities, it still fails to address the wonderful
stones cut to nonstandard shapes. This article
answers that need. The technique described
here makes it possible to create a stonesetting without soldering, offering artists without
metalworking skills a way to incorporate their
stone cabs into beautiful silver jewelry.

BACKGROUND

Over and over again, I tried to make settings
entirely out of PMC for my cabochon stones.
They never worked out to my satisfaction,
and in my frustration, I'd let some time go by
before I'd make another attempt. Instead, I
experimented with glass cabs fired in place,
limiting my gem selection to stones that
would stand up to PMC3 schedules, or simply
working with the clay on its own. Still, I was
restless, always glancing over at my growing
collection of unique and beautiful stone cabs.

Ultimately I was compelled to try and
make it work with PMC, even if just to say it
could be done. Shrinkage was the main issue.
I needed a way to figure out how much big-
ger to make the setting so the stone would fit
it perfectly after firing. My patience was also
an issue, as I didn't want to take the time to
make a mold of my stone, then make a paper
maché footprint to help the PMC retain its
correct size.

After a good bit of experimentation, I have developed a system that works consistently. Here is a summary of the steps, each of which is described in detail below:

- Create a template adjusted for pre-fired size
- Ornament the base
- Create a bezel using PMC Paper
- Attach the bezel
- Fire
- Set the stone
- Finish

First I scan a cab and increase the size to compensate for shrinkage. Then I print the image and use it as an exact template to make my setting. It occurred to me that PMC Paper might be great to use for a bezel wall, and through a trial and error process, I found a way to make it work. I have set over one hundred stones now, from very big to very small, using this method.

Wherever possible, it is best to set the stone face down when making an image. If the stone is very tall or irregular, this might not be possible. In that case, set the stone on its bottom, but remember which side is up as you work through the process.

a) Using a Photocopier

Place your cabochon on the glass of a copier, set the Enlarge button to 118% and press Start. The actual shrinkage is about 15%, and to end up with this reduction, we need to start with something larger than 100%. I like to set the stone face down, because this makes it easier to visualize the stone throughout the process. If the stone is tall, set it right side up on the glass to avoid the tilt that will come when the lid is closed.

Print the enlarged image and cut it out precisely with good quality scissors. This paper template will be your guide in making the bezel, so time spent here will be repaid throughout the rest of the process.

Use a photocopier to create an enlarged image of your stone. The goal is to calculate the size and shape for a PMC bezel that will fit the stone after shrinking.

Journey Necklace (detail)
Fine silver, sterling, ammonite
2" diameter

Reversible Shell Pendant
Fine silver, shell, sterling. 1¾" diameter
The bezel is made from PMC Paper that has been textured.

b) Using a Scanner

Place the stone on a flatbed scanner and scan it at 118%. Print the enlarged image of the stone and cut it out precisely. This paper template of your stone will guide you in making your bezel. You could also adjust the size in the printing step: scan at 100% and print at 118%.

About the Numbers

To calculate shrinkage, take 100% (i.e., full size) minus 15% shrinkage. Divide this by the 100% you want to achieve and you'll get 118%.

$$100-15=85$$
$$100÷.85=118$$

An alternate method is to scan the stone and resize the image on a computer. Both methods result in the same thing; the choice of which to use depends entirely on your equipment and personal preference.

MAKING THE BACKSHEET

Roll out a piece of PMC+ or PMC3 to a thickness of three cards for a large stone, and two cards for a small stone, (say under a half inch wide). I like to texture what will be the back side of the bezel, but this will vary depending on your design needs.

Cut out a piece of PMC that will be a little larger than the finished bezel. Set the paper template onto the PMC sheet and cut a line about a millimeter outside the edge of the template with a needle. If your stone is symmetrical, like a circle or an oval, it doesn't matter whether the template or the sheet is right side up. If the stone is irregular, and the sheet has a textured (back) side, make sure you pay attention to the proper orientation. Set the piece aside to air dry.

When the backsheet is dry, place the template on it (again paying attention to orientation if the stone is asymmetrical) and sand the edge. The goal here is to create a panel that is the exact footprint of the stone. In this construction, the bezel will be attached to the outside edge of the backsheet. Metalsmiths will recognize that this is contrary to traditional practice, where bezels are soldered on top of the sheet. If the backsheet and template dont match precisely, the stone won't fit in the bezel. This step is really important to insure a good fit.

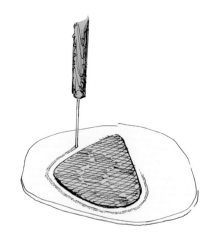

Roll out a sheet of PMC a little larger than the stone template to become the backsheet. Lay the paper template on the PMC and cut slightly outside the template with a needle.

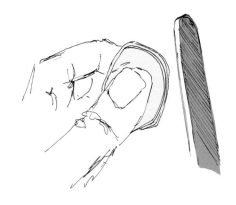

After the backsheet has dried, use a sanding stick to make the form exactly match the template.

THE BEZEL WALL

In order to hold a stone securely, a bezel needs to reach over the curve of a stone so it can pinch the stone down onto the base. In order to make the setting smooth and easy, the bezel should not have more material than can be easily compressed. In other words, bezels need to be tall enough but not too tall. Of the two choices, too tall is preferred because it is easy to correct.

Determine the height of the bezel wall by looking carefully at the profile of the stone. Visualize the finished height of the bezel, and add a little bit to account for shrinkage. With experience, most people find they can get the

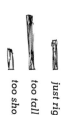

The proper height for a bezel depends on the individual stone. If the stone is shallow, a low bezel will hold it securely, but if the stone is tall or unevenly cut, a taller bezel will be needed.

too short *too tall* *just right*

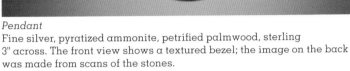

Pendant
Fine silver, pyratized ammonite, petrified palmwood, sterling
3" across. The front view shows a textured bezel; the image on the back
was made from scans of the stones.

right height by eye, but if it helps, hold a stiff
paper beside the stone and make a pencil
mark at the point where the stone starts to
curve away from the point of contact. Make
the bezel at least two millimeters taller than
this mark (one millimeter to allow sufficient
height and one for the base).

The next step is to cut out a strip of PMC
Paper for the bezel. To avoid making it too
short or too narrow, take a minute to cut a
strip of paper to what you think is the right
size. Wrap this around the prepared backsheet. Leave the strip about three millimeters
too long to provide for overlap of the joint.

Mark and cut a piece of PMC Paper with
a tissue blade, a craft knife, or scissors. In
both length and width, it is better to err on the
generous side, but not by much. Careful mea-
surement is an easy habit to master, and it
will save both time and money when the strip
is close to the needed size. Sand a bevel onto
each end of the strip—this will allow the seam
to overlap without creating a section that has
double thickness.

Use a strip of paper to measure
the length needed for the bezel.

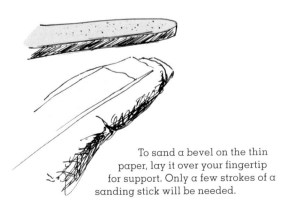

To sand a bevel on the thin
paper, lay it over your fingertip
for support. Only a few strokes of a
sanding stick will be needed.

ATTACHING THE WALL TO THE BACKSHEET

If you have not worked with PMC Paper before, take two minutes and 20¢ worth of Paper for an important lesson. Cut a piece about an eighth inch on each side, and add a generous brushful of water. Wait a few seconds and poke the PMC Paper with your finger or a scribe. You'll see that it has the strength and texture of wet tissue paper. You'll reflect that this is not what a bezel should look like. OK, good to know.

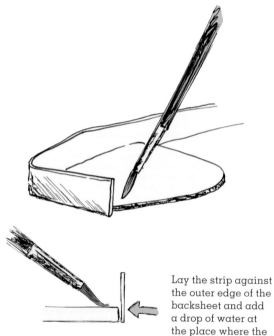

Armed with this knowledge, you are now ready to attach the PMC Paper strip to the edge of the backsheet. Set the backsheet on a piece of Teflon or a playing card, which makes it easy to rotate the piece as you work. Set the bezel strip around the sheet, standing on edge. Use your index finger to press the PMC Paper against the backsheet, with your other hand, touch the tip of a dampened paintbrush to the seam where the PMC Paper touches the edge of the sheet. Capillary action will pull water into the seam instantly. Move along the piece and repeat the process, adding water to the joint every quarter-inch or so. Too much water and the PMC Paper will disintegrate; too little and the PMC Paper won't attach to the backsheet. When you have worked your way around the bezel, dampen the beveled surfaces of the seam and overlap the ends. Set the piece aside to dry, either naturally, or with the help of a hydrator or heat source.

Lay the strip against the outer edge of the backsheet and add a drop of water at the place where the two meet. Use a finger to press the bezel against the sheet, advancing around the sheet.

When the bezel is dry, refine the edges and seams by trimming, sanding, and smoothing with a damp brush. Hold the bezel with your thumb and index finger pinching the backsheet, so you don't accidentally squash the fragile bezel wall. Trim excess paper off the back of the bezel with a knife and smooth the seams around the base with a damp brush. Smooth over the area where the bezel ends join, working on both the inside and the outside. To refine the edge, grip the piece so the bezel wall is supported on your thumbnail and sand gently with a light grit paper. The goal is to make the line disappear, but don't worry if the result is not perfect—you can sand it further after firing.

Set the bezel aside to dry again. At this point, it can be added to any sort of PMC object. In some designs, I start with a bezel and add parts around it. In others, I make the piece first, then attach a bezel that has been made according to the method just described.

Fire the piece flat on a kiln shelf at 1650° (900° C) for 30 minutes.

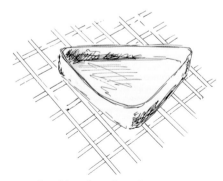

Set the completed bezel aside to dry, naturally, on a heated surface, or in a dehydrator.

SETTING THE STONE

Shrinkage during firing will cause your bezel wall to slant inward. To correct this, use the rounded end of a paintbrush handle (or any similar soft blunt tool) to ease the bezel outward. Roll the tool around the inside of the bezel while exerting a gentle outward pressure. Avoid the temptation to test the fit by forcing the stone into place. If you need to lay the stone lightly on the bezel to examine the fit, lay a piece of dental floss over the bezel first. If the stone drops into place, the string will make it easier to retrieve.

Before setting the stone, drill holes, add findings, etc. Actual finishing of the bezel wall will be done after the stone is set—in this way the stone itself provides support for the finishing process. Before pressing the stone into place, make a final determination about the bezel height. Hold the stone beside the bezel and raise it to eye level. Careful observation will reveal whether you have too much bezel, not enough, or just the right amount. If the bezel is not high enough, well… that's bad. Sometimes you can use a lower stone, but the options are definitely limited. If the height is just right, good job. If the bezel is too high, you have two options, both good. You can trim the bezel down, which is easily done with manicure scissors. Or, you can raise the stone by inserting a piece of thin cardboard. Trace the stone onto paper (I use matchbook cardboard), cut inside the line with scissors, and drop the lift into the bezel. Use as many layers as necessary.

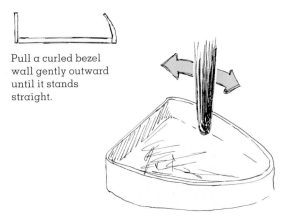

Pull a curled bezel wall gently outward until it stands straight.

It often happens that bezels get pressed inward through normal handling. To pull the bezel back to an upright position, use a small smooth tool like a paintbrush handle. Pull it out, but not so far that it curls outward.

Journey Necklace
Fine silver, sterling, serpentine, shell, button, ammonite
Center piece is 2" diameter

Check the bezel height again, but not by pressing the stone into the bezel, where it might get stuck. Instead, set the stone beside the bezel. If the bezel is too high, either cut the strip with scissors or add a layer or two of thin cardboard to raise the stone up.

Here's the trick of stonesetting: When the bezel is a good fit and properly prepared, the setting process is remarkably easy. Assuming you've reached this point, drop the stone into place and press down firmly to insure that it is well seated. Setting proceeds as with traditional metalsmithing. Use a blunt rod of steel, brass, or hard plastic to press the bezel onto the stone. Commercial bezel pushers are nothing more than a square steel rod set into a bulbous handle. A nail in a rounded block of wood, or a sawn off toothbrush handle will also work. The goal is to lean the bezel against the stone without leaving marks.

Journey Necklace (reverse)

If soldering is needed, it must be done before setting the stone. Otherwise, insert the stone and use a bezel pusher to press the bezel over the stone.

If you were to start at one place and work your way around, you would end up with a gather of metal at the end that would leave an unsightly lump. To avoid this, work back and forth across the bezel. It doesn't matter where you start, but if you think of the stone as a clock face, this would be a typical sequence: 12, 6, 3, 9. Continue in this way until the bezel lays smooth and the stone is gripped tightly.

I usually finish my settings with a brass brush. Burnishers and brassbrushes will not hurt gems, but abrasive papers will, so work carefully to avoid marring the stone. Add patina if desired.

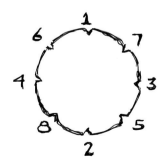

To avoid a pucker or bulge, move sequentially around the bezel, hopping back and forth to distribute the compression.

VARIATIONS

USING PMC3 INSTEAD OF PMC PAPER

In most cases, I prefer using PMC Paper for bezels, but there is an alternative and it has some advantages worth mentioning. If you choose to roll out a very thin sheet of PMC3 to use as a bezel, you are not handicapped by the size of PMC Paper. Also, the flexibility of the Paper is a mixed blessing, leaving the bezel fragile until after firing. The disadvantage of making your own sheet is that it is not as flexible, and therefore not as easy to wrap around the backsheet. Also, it does not adhere to the backsheet quite as readily.

We usually use playing cards to determine thickness, but even one card is too thick for most bezels. Instead, for this process I use three layers of standard copy paper, cutting strips to a convenient size. It is difficult to form a bezel when the clay has just been rolled out because the PMC will flop over rather than stand upright. Instead, roll out a strip for the bezel, set it aside to dry, then refresh it by painting a bit of water on one side. Allow a few minutes for this to soak in, and you'll find that the strip is now relatively flexible. Proceed as before, remoistening again if the bezel becomes stiff.

MAKING A TEXTURED BEZEL

This variation can be used on bezels made from PMC Paper and from PMC3 as just described. In both cases, keep the texture shallow. Deep texture areas will weaken the bezel and make it difficult to achieve a smooth bend. Also, a dramatic texture will be difficult to press over the stone. Set as usual, but use the burnisher carefully so you don't erase or blunt the texture.

METAL SHOWING AROUND THE STONE

Some designs call for a rim of silver around the stone. To accomplish this, first make the backsheet in the intended size, larger than the stone by whatever amount you want to show. When the panel is dry, locate the template on the sheet and trace around it with a needle. Extrude a line of Syringe PMC just inside this line, anchoring it in place with a damp brush. When dry, this ridge will provide a stop against which you can attach the bezel as described above.

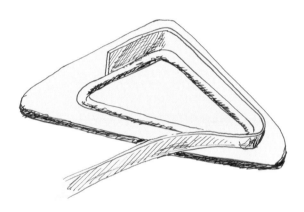

To anchor a bezel on a backsheet so that some of the sheet shows around the stone, scribe a line around the template then extrude a thread from a PMC Syringe just inside that line. Blend into the base with a damp brush, allow to dry, then press a PMC Paper bezel against it. Don't make the extruded line too large or it will be difficult to set the stone.

TROUBLESHOOTING

What can I do if the backsheet warps?

Brush or spritz water onto the untextured side of the panel and allow 30–60 seconds for it to penetrate. Sandwich the PMC between two pieces of Teflon or plastic sheet, and set this under the Collegiate Edition, Merriam-Webster Dictionary, Third Edition—or a similar book. After about twenty minutes, you'll find that the sheet has flattened. Lift the book and plastic away and allow the piece to dry for another ten minutes before handling.

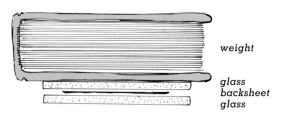

weight

glass
backsheet
glass

If the backsheet warps, dampen it slightly and press it between flat surfaces under a weight.

You can double the thickness of PMC Paper by laminating two sheets together. Spritz or otherwise gently moisten two sheets and lay them one on top of the other. Caress with your fingers to smooth out air bubbles and excess water and apply gentle pressure while the sheets dry, for instance by setting a book onto the stack. It is possible to laminate up to four layers, but I would limit bezels to two.

How do I make a long strip of PMC Paper?

Large stones might require a length of bezel that exceeds the PMC Paper you have on hand. To splice two strips together seamlessly, file a bevel on the end of two matching strips. This is a delicate operation, which I do by supporting the strip against my fingertip. Moisten the bevels slightly with water and overlap the strips. Paint with a damp brush to seal the joint, then set the strip aside to dry. Resist the urge to pick it up before the clay is completely bonded, (at least ten minutes). Once dry, sand the edges to make the seam disappear.

To make a long strip, bevel the ends of two strips, dampen them slightly, and press them together.

Doris King

Fusing Sterling Silver to PMC

I came to metals from a background in painting and textile design. Maybe because of that, I am always looking for techniques that allow me to work with metals in a painterly way. I have spent hours sawing out patterns, stamping, reticulating, using the rolling mill, and soldering in an effort to add color, texture and dimension to my designs. I was introduced to PMC in 1999, and it took me a while to get comfortable with this metal in clay form. I was used to hammering metal, and PMC needed a gentler touch. Once I learned the techniques and discovered how PMC could create texture and dimension in metal, I was hooked. Now I think of PMC as another jewelry technique, a new way of working with metal that allows me to sculpt directly, showing my touch in the metal itself.

BACKGROUND

In the beginning there was fine silver. Actually, fine gold and copper came first, but many hundreds of years ago, artists worked with pure silver. The metal was almost unbeatable for workability, luster, and shine. But works made of pure silver could be easily scratched and bent. After generations of trial and error, it was discovered that a small amount of copper added to the silver created an alloy that was stronger and tougher while retaining most of the desirable properties of the pure metal. Around 600 years ago, this alloy became standardized at 7½% copper and picked up the name "sterling." A 600-year track record tells us that sterling has a lot to offer.

Precious Metal Clay brings immediacy and design possibilities that have never existed before. In an effort to get the best of both materials, I began to experiment with ways to join PMC to sterling. Along the way, I enlisted the help of my students. Limited thinking was out—imagination was in. Curiosity and creativity were at their best. I appreciate this collective effort and I am excited to share our discoveries.

Benefits of combining sterling and PMC

Before looking at how we combine these metals, let's look at the why. It will be helpful to understand the contrasting benefits and drawbacks of each, and then we can look at the practical reasons why practicing artists are interested in the possibilities.

	Benefits	Disadvantages
Sterling	• strong • relatively cheap • available in many forms (findings, shanks, settings) • can be hardened	• it will tarnish • requires serious tools to work • requires training & experience • limited to sheet & wire • soldering creates firescale
PMC	• easy to work • needs only simple tools • slow to tarnish	• soft • relatively expensive • does not workharden

Advantages

Here are a few of the benefits of using PMC and sterling together. Your situation and design choices might suggest others. Joining sterling and PMC without solder saves the cost of soldering equipment and the space required to do the soldering.

• Sterling costs less than PMC, not only because it contains some copper, but because the technology to create and process it has been around for centuries. In addition, using ready-made components like ring shanks or stone settings reduces the overall time required to make a piece, and this translates to a greater profit in the marketplace.

• PMC is easily textured and shaped, and the tools needed for PMC are inexpensive and easily found or made. Texturing and forming sterling requires additional and expensive tools, time, and skills.

• Sales may increase because the combination of these metals results in a unique product. The general public is familiar with sterling silver. Combining sterling with PMC might help others understand and accept PMC as well.

APPLICATIONS

Metal clay is simply terrific for capturing textures, generating forms, and modeling. Compared to the demanding and time-consuming methods required in traditional metalwork, PMC offers ease, speed, and expressive opportunity. Sterling, on the other hand, is the best choice for strength, or when you need clean planar surfaces, for instance in box construction or under flat-backed stones. Each person will find different ways to use sterling and PMC for his or her specific needs, but let me suggest a few possibilities.

I like to make bracelets, and because fine silver is a poor choice for bangle bracelets, I use sterling for the cuff of the bracelets I make. In a similar way, I use sterling for ring shanks, and then embellish them with PMC ornaments. Using sterling in this way not only provides the desired strength, but also eliminates the sizing challenge that arises when using PMC. Sterling is generally preferred when a small amount of metal needs to carry a lot of stress, as for instance in findings, but even these can benefit from PMC additions. I sometimes embellish commercial, generic-looking sterling pendant bails with PMC to coordinate with the design of a pendant.

The question to ask yourself is this: What is the best way to achieve my goal here? Is this need best met with the plasticity of PMC or the uniformity and strength of sterling?

People with a background in metalsmithing are likely at this point to turn to soldering or rivets to join PMC to sterling, and those two options have dominated the field so far. I am proposing three alternative solutions, none of which require the skills or equipment of traditional metalsmithing. They will be explained below, but first we should discuss proper preparation of the sterling.

A Celebration of Blue & Green
PMC clay, syringe, and slip, sterling low-dome wire and bezel cups, parrot wing agate, gaspeite, turquoise

DEPLETION GILDING

Because of the copper content in sterling silver, the metal will oxidize (tarnish) quickly when it is heated. This gray skin of silver and copper oxides (AgO_2 and Cu_2O) inhibits or even prevents parts from fusing together. A solution is to remove the copper from the surface of the sterling alloy to leave a layer of fine silver that will not oxidize. The effect is to coat or "gild" the metal, and because this is achieved by leaching out or depleting the copper, the process is called depletion gilding.

Depletion gilding has been used historically in various ways. It will be familiar to metalsmiths from its use in keum-boo and reticulation. For centuries, metal artists

Pickle works at room temperature, but the process is accelerated with moderate heat. A convenient way to keep pickle warm is with a crock pot.

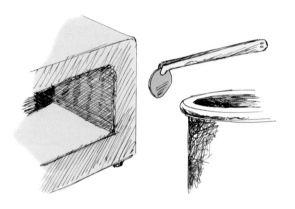

To convert copper in sterling to copper oxide, heat the metal, either with a torch or, as shown, in a kiln.

have used this inventive process as a final step in finishing to leave a tarnish-resistant layer of pure silver on their sterling wares. The process consists of creating oxides on the surface then immersing the work in an acid solution called pickle that dissolves the copper oxides to leave a thin layer of pure silver. This fine silver layer is compatible with PMC and they will fuse.

Depletion gilding is traditionally done with a torch, but in an effort to simplify the process and eliminate additional equipment, I use my PMC kiln. Before describing the process, let me say a word about pickle.

The most commonly used pickle nowadays is a proprietary product called Sparex (sodium bisulfate). This is sold as granules that are dissolved in warm water to make a mildly acidic solution. Historically, a 10 to 1 mixture of water and sulfuric acid was used, but Sparex is preferred because it is much less caustic. Alternatives include pH lowering chemicals sold at pool and spa stores (active ingredient: sodium bisulfate), and, getting historical again, vinegar, which is where the name comes from. All pickles work at room temperature, but all of them work faster if heated to bath water temperatures. Most studios do this in a crock pot, but a saucepan on an electric coil also works.

I recommend depletion gilding for all the joining processes described below, so it is appropriate to describe the steps here.

Turquoise Rainbow
Sterling wire and
bezel cups, PMC
slip and syringe,
turquoise

STEPS FOR DEPLETION GILDING

1 Saw, bend, file, and shape the sterling element. Score and drill holes if they will be needed (explained below).

2 Put the sterling in a cold kiln. Program the kiln to ramp up at full speed and hold at 1200° F (650 °C) for five minutes.

3 Remove the sterling from the kiln after the five minutes, and allow it to cool slightly. Drop the sterling into a pickle solution (Sparex) for about five minutes, until the metal turns white.

4 Remove the sterling from the pickle solution with copper or plastic tongs, rinse with water, and scrub the sterling with a brass brush. Brassbrushing strengthens the bond between the fine silver layer and the sterling beneath.

5 Return the sterling to the kiln and heat it again to 1200° F (650° C), this time holding for ten minutes.

6 Pickle again for five minutes, rinse in water, and brassbrush.

SURFACE FUSING

In certain limited situations, it is possible to simply apply PMC elements onto prepared sterling and fire the pieces together. In practice, this requires that the pieces have a sufficient surface area to support the joint. An earring post standing vertically up from a surface, for example, could not be attached this way. A line of syringe or a layer of PMC applied to sterling to enrich the surface offers more area to fuse to the sterling, which is what we want.

Fine silver, like fine gold, has a natural desire to bond with itself. If the conditions are right, all that is required is to heat the components and they will join together as if by magic. I draw with slip or syringe on depletion gilded sterling with no scoring, and the bond is secure as long as the surface is clean and the contact is absolutely solid. The trick here is to see that there is nothing chemical preventing the two parts from swapping electrons. Copper oxide will prevent this, and so will finger oils, dust, dirt, and soap. Beside the condition of cleanliness, the other condition that needs to be met is to insure that the parts are in close contact. And because we're talking about a joint at the crystalline level, this contact needs to be very, very tight.

Roughen the surfaces of both parts by scratching with a needle, a file, or coarse sandpaper. Next, raise the fine silver skin by depletion gilding as described above, handling the pieces only by their edges or with tweezers to preserve cleanliness.

To make a perfect joint, paint a bit of PMC slip (or squirt a dollop of PMC Syringe) onto the PMC piece, then press the pieces together. Like a brick pressing into mortar, this semi-liquid material will mold itself to the contours of both pieces and insure a perfect fit. Allow the slip to dry, then fire as usual. This method is acceptable for small pieces, but it is not recommended for elements that stand high enough to be exposed to wear and tear.

Embellished Bangle
PMC syringe, slip,
and clay, sterling half-round
wire, turquoise, sponge coral

MECHANICAL CONNECTIONS

The definition of a mechanical connection is a physical attachment between two parts. A staple is an example of a mechanical connection, as is a nut and bolt, or the prongs used to hold a gem in place. In all these cases, one part physically presses down on another, and the strength of the holding element locks the pieces together.

Small sterling elements can be embedded in PMC, and if properly done, this method will exploit two connection devices—the fusing just described and the mechanical grip that happens when one component curls over another. Imagine attaching a bezel cup, prong setting, or sterling casting into an object made of PMC (or to another sterling piece, using PMC as the joint). If you simply press the parts together, they might join, but they might not. If, however, you design the sterling element so it has a bevel, a ledge, or a handle that can be gripped by the PMC as it shrinks, this grip is guaranteed. By gilding the sterling so it has a skin of fine silver, the points of contact are almost certain to fuse together. Using this in conjunction with a mechanical grip guarantees a permanent union.

This method works especially well for small dimensional elements, such as small bezel cups or sterling shapes applied as ornaments. In situations like these, score the back of the sterling pieces, raise the fine silver by depletion gilding, then lay the parts on a bed of PMC slip. I like to score the base piece as well, just to insure that the PMC has tooth to grab onto. Use enough slip so that it will squeeze up around the edges of the form. When the PMC is fired, it will shrink and grip the piece securely. In the case of a bezel, don't allow the PMC to reach more than a third of the way up the side. This is sufficient to make a strong joint, but not so much that it will make it difficult to press the bezel over the stone.

You can use commercial slip or paste that you make yourself, but I prefer to use Syringe PMC3 because I have better control with this material. You'll want to experiment to find out what works best for you.

For an even stronger joint, provide a way for the PMC to reach through a piece. In this example, a layer of slip will help to hold a sterling bezel cup in place, but by drilling holes in the floor of the cup, that joint is reinforced by fused rivets created when the PMC oozes through the holes.

After firing, the PMC solidifies into a rivet head that will lock the parts together.

It Works!
Fine silver bezel wire, sterling sheet, PMC syringe, clay, and slip,
ammonite, turquoise, sugilite, and gaspeite

BASIC FUSED RIVET

Perhaps the most common mechanical connection used in jewelry is a rivet—a short
segment of wire that runs through two or
more pieces and has a bulge on each end.
Traditionally, these are made by hammering
the ends of wire, but PMC offers a simple and
exciting alternative that I call a fused rivet.

Drill holes in the sterling at the point of
connection. The holes can be small — one
or two millimeters is enough to allow PMC
slip to ooze through. This is what will make
a PMC rivet after firing. The number of holes
depends on the element you are connecting
and the amount of stress the joint will need
to withstand. One hole may be enough if the
element is small, but you should use several if a strong joint is needed. Imagine, for
instance, a sterling bezel cup that will hold a
tall stone onto a ring. Because of the height of
the stone and the way rings can be accidentally knocked about, this situation calls for a
particularly strong joint. I would drill at least
four holes in the base of the bezel cup, and
more if there is room. It might help to think
of these rivets as nails. If you are hanging a
picture, one nail might be enough, but if you
are constructing a shipping crate, you won't
spare the nails.

EXAMPLE

Imagine a ring shank made from a band of sterling. Before pressing the PMC component into place, I will drill a couple small holes in both ends of the shank. Work proceeds as usual, but now I am confident that the PMC will not only fuse to the surface, but will grab onto the sterling with a finger of metal that locks the parts together.

BRIDGING A GAP

I mentioned earlier that one of the situations where sterling is commonly used with PMC is for bracelets and ring shanks. In both these cases, the sterling is bent into a circle, and, in conventional fabrication, the joint is closed with solder. Using PMC for the ornament not only provides the aesthetics of metal clay at the top of the ring or bracelet, but can simultaneously close the band. A strong joint can be made by engineering a mechanical grip, which I'll illustrate with two examples.

A ring shank drilled for fused rivets.

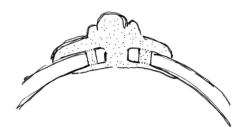

To attach parts on a wire, file a rough notch on the end and press the PMC over it. When the metal clay shrinks, it will both fuse and mechanically bond.

Harmonic Contrasts
Sterling bezel cup and cast ring shank, fine silver bezel, PMC syringe, slip, and clay, ammonite, dichroic glass

EXAMPLE

Let's think now of a bracelet made from a length of six gauge sterling round wire. It would be difficult to drill holes through such a sturdy wire, and I'm not certain the PMC would ooze all the way through. Instead, I'll file a bevel around the wire. You might picture the notch on the arrowheads we learned about as children. Simply tying a triangular piece of stone onto a shaft would not do, so the arrowheads have an indent that holds the thread. In this case the indent will go all the way around the bracelet shank—it does not need to be particularly smooth or attractive, nor does it need to be deep, but it should be easy to feel with your fingernail. I smooth a good bit of PMC3 slip onto the sterling to insure that the space between the carved sterling and the fresh PMC is filled. The PMC will shrink into this recess, burying it from sight as it makes a firm mechanical grip between the silver ornament and the sterling bracelet.

FIRING SCHEDULES

Original PMC needs to be fired at 1650° F (900° C) for two hours. When sterling is held at that temperature for that long, it might reticulate, and it will certainly become brittle. The solution, when using Original PMC, is to fire the metal clay elements first, then attach them to sterling with PMC3. Though PMC+ fires for a shorter time and at a lower temperature, I also recommend firing PMC+ before attaching it to the sterling.

In most cases, the reason to combine PMC with sterling is to gain the benefit of sterling's strength, so it makes sense to preserve this strength if we can. And we can. I recommend firing at 1350° F (730° C) for 30 minutes. At this temperature, the sterling remains strong and resilient. There is a slight increase in the heat hardening of the sterling after firing at this temperature, although sterling sheet and wires can still be shaped without difficulty.

Alchemist's Mark
Sterling gallery wire, bead wire, and bezel cups, PMC, turquoise

PMC3 can be attached to sterling as fresh, dry, or fired PMC. I prefer to use PMC3 fresh and apply it directly to the sterling. In this state, the PMC3 can be easily manipulated to fit the shape of your sterling elements.

When working with sterling that is 24 gauge or thinner, I recommend firing for 20 minutes at 1200° F (650° C). Thinner metals achieve a secure fusion at this lower temperature and shorter time and this reduced schedule counteracts the tendency of this piece to warp during firing.

Soldered pieces require special mention, since there is another metal present (the solder). If you are firing a piece that has been previously soldered, and if you do not know for sure what kind of solder was used, I recommend firing at 1200° F 650° C) to be safely under the melting point of all solders.

CONCLUSION

Combining sterling and PMC opens the door for unique design opportunities. PMC offers artists the ability to mold shapes and embellish sterling with design elements, stones, and texture in a way that shows the hand of the artist directly in the metal. Sterling also provides strength for the structure of the piece as well as convenience because of the availability and variety of sterling components, sheet, and wire. The challenge of bringing the best of these materials and the techniques they offer provides fuel for innovation and discovery.

Sleeping Beauty & Moonstone Bracelet
Sterling silver low-dome wire, PMC syringe, slip, and clay, fine silver bezel wire, carved turquoise and moonstone

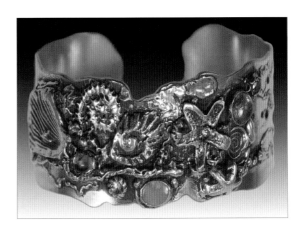

Treasure Hunt
Sterling sheet (18 gauge), sterling bezel cups, PMC syringe, slip, and clay, opal, peridot, CZs, and dichroic glass

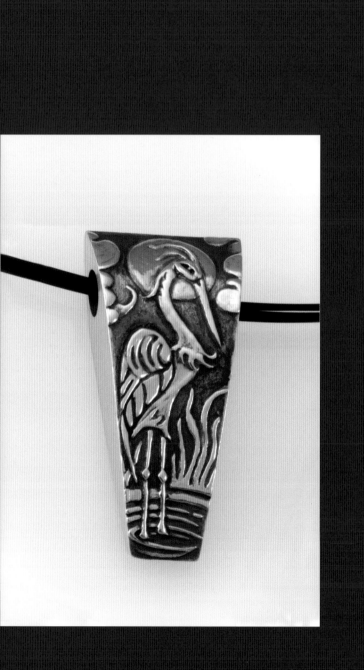

Terry Kovalcik

Developing Form with Slip

For many people, slip is used to glue PMC parts together, and while it can do this, there are other possibilities too. One example is using PMC slip as a surface treatment. It's possible to spread slip like frosting on a cake, but I am more interested in a controlled application, which is what I will discuss here.

The term "viscosity" refers to the gooeyness of a material, and in this case, the thickness of the PMC slip will influence the process and the results you will get. Viscosity can be adjusted by adding water, or by allowing the slip to dry out a little. To master this technique and to really make it your own, experiment with slip of various consistencies to see the varying effects you can achieve.

Viscosity painting will work with all versions of metal clay, but I prefer PMC3 Slip. It builds up fastest and yields a tougher result than the others. Original PMC spreads out further when applied because of its higher proportion of water. Slip made from Original PMC is appropriate for amorphous, soft-edged ornaments, or when applying to a base of Original because it will alleviate distortion problems that will result with a slip that did not match shrinkage.

Firing work that has been ornamented with this technique follows the time and temperature schedules provided by the manufacturer, but remember that the nature of slip is that it contains a lot more water than normal metal clay. Be sure to allow the work to dry completely before firing.

BACKROUND

As someone with a background in illustration and painting, I enjoy the feel of a brush to lay down a line, in this case a line of paste. For about twenty-five years, I've made my living as an illustrator. My illustrations use airbrush techniques, and usually include a lot of detail… I guess some people would call it compulsive. I love to spend a lot of time working over a small space, refining edges and lines with obsessive precision. An illustration job required that I make something in polymer clay, and that got me interested in polymer clay as a creative outlet. Working in three-dimensions led me to PMC, and I guess it was only a matter of time before my two careers—developing form and ornamenting surfaces—came together.

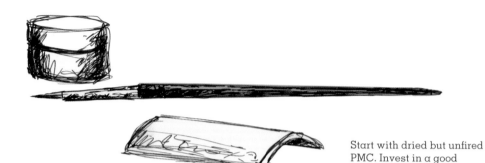

Start with dried but unfired PMC. Invest in a good quality brush, and avoid homemade slip.

PREPARATION

The first step is to create a "canvas" on which to deposit the slip. This can be constructed in any of the familiar ways we work with PMC, by rolling, carving, layering, and so on. This technique works on fired or unfired PMC, but the bond between slip and metal does not always hold. If you are working on fired PMC, leave the surface matte to improve the grip. Better yet, apply the slip to unfired PMC, where the probability of fusing is 100%. You can draw the design directly onto the surface lightly with a pencil or you can work free-hand. In the case of complicated designs and images, you might want to draw it on paper first, then transfer it using carbon paper.

Fine silver and sterling findings. The boxes were made with PMC Paper and Clay; the ornamentation is all made with slip.
2" high

Getting the viscosity right

Viscosity, or the thickness of the slip, is a key to making this process enjoyable and successful. The goal is to achieve a viscosity that is fluid enough to ooze gracefully from the brush, but stiff enough that it will stay where you place it. The stiffer the slip (that is, the less water), the faster it will dry, and this speeds up the process. I always start with factory-made slip. Of course I recycle my PMC scraps into slip and that's fine for many purposes, but for ease of application and a smooth result, I rely on slip that I'm sure is free of lint, pet hair, crumbs, and the other studio debris that might be in my homemade batch. Luscious as it is, the factory slip is too thick to trail nicely, so the first step is to add a little water. How much? That's difficult to capture in words, but I can offer a test. Open a jar of slip and stick a toothpick into it, straight up. I think you'll find that it remains in that position. Now add a few drops of water and stir well. Try the test again: if the toothpick still stands up, add a little more water. Continue in this way until you find the point where it falls over by itself. Voila! If I had to describe these two consistencies in food terms, I'd say the commercial slip is like yogurt, and what we want is like a yogurt drink.

Here's another way to tell: With the proper consistency, you should be able to draw out a line that is at least a quarter-inch long. If your lines are shorter than that, the slip is probably too thick. After some experimentation, you'll find your own comfort zone.

Slip as it comes from the factory is too thick for painting. A toothpick in commercial slip will stand up on its own. Add a few drops of water and stir well, then test with a toothpick again. The proper consistency will allow the toothpick to slowly fall down.

Fine silver and sterling
1½" high

PAINTING WITH SLIP

Use a fine brush with a point size of #00, 0, or 1. A simple way to determine the quality of a brush is to look at the price. Don't waste your time on anything that costs less than five dollars. I find that the better your brush can hold a sharp tip, the better the results when laying down the paste. A top quality brush not only makes for a nicer result, but makes the process faster and easier too.

To start, dip the brush in water, flick it to remove most of the moisture, then carefully twirl the tip into a point on the side of your hand. Dip into the paste jar just to no more than half the height of the bristles. That is, don't load too much slip onto your brush, and definitely don't allow it to get up onto the ferrule. Touch the tip of the loaded brush to the surface you are going to decorate, then lift it slightly. Pull out a line of paste by allowing the brush to float slowly a few millimeters above the surface. The process is difficult to describe in words, but, like riding a bike, it's easy to know when you get it right. In this case, control and the gracefulness of the line are achieved by coordinating the viscosity of the slip, the angle of the brush, and the speed of the stroke. And it helps if you haven't loaded up on coffee… Allow yourself some time to experiment until you get the results you want.

Practice is always a good idea. Here are a couple test panels I recommend. Once you can lay down a line that has consistent width, and you can control the shape of the mark, you are ready to work on finished objects.

I find that I fall into a rhythm as work proceeds. When the thread of slip starts to thin, or the pace at which it leaves the brush slows down, gather another droplet of slip on the tip of the brush, again taking care that you don't load up too much. Carefully touch the tip of the brush to the end point of the line and continue laying down a thread of slip, often moving the work as much as the brush to steer the tendril of wet slip to its intended location on the PMC base. Twirling the brush seems to help in laying down a longer line, but even with this trick, you'll find that each droplet makes only a short line. When the droplet on the end of the brush is used up, go back for more and continue to add to the line. Here's an important tip: If the slip starts to dry on the tip of the brush or to migrate up toward the ferrule (which will cause the hairs to spread), it is time to rinse out the brush. Keep a small cup of water handy for this purpose. The excess PMC slip will sink to the bottom of the cup as silt that can be recovered later. Don't put off cleaning the brush as soon as the slip begins to dry. It is important to keep a sharp, unclogged tip on the brush for maximum flow and line control.

When you have laid down a single line over the entire drawing, it probably won't look like much. Let it dry, then lay an additional line on top of the first one. Continue in this way, adding more layers to develop a raised line. Depending on the design, it is not unusual to apply between three and seven layers—sometimes even more. It is important to allow each layer to dry completely before laying down the next one. Moving too quickly risks losing a crisp line and often leads to a lack of control. I find that the first couple lines tend to spread a little, widening the base. As the lines dry, you might notice tiny bubbles or slumped areas. Fill these in as you move along with an extra dab here and there.

Each number corresponds to the number of layers used to make it

To create a solid area, for instance a circle or a triangle, start by laying down a line that describes the shape you want to make. When it dries, this will act as a dam that surrounds an interior space that you will fill with slip. The larger the area being filled, the more it is likely that the slip will slump in its center as it dries. Just fill in those slumped areas with additional slip, letting each layer dry between coats.

Fine silver, sterling. PMC3 slip is used to make the ornamentation on the dome. 2¼" high

Fine silver, sterling, pearls
2³/₈" high

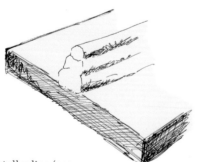

To create a taller line (or a wall), lay a couple lines down on top of each other. Always allow a line to dry before adding to it.

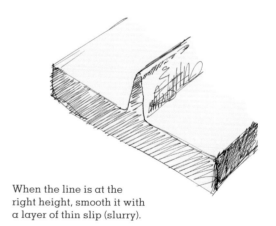

When the line is at the right height, smooth it with a layer of thin slip (slurry).

Once you have achieved the desired affect (in this case the depth of the line, or height of the wall), the final step is to give the entire surface a coat or two of thinned paste that I will call slurry. Again, viscosity is the name of the game here, and experimentation is recommended. It is very important to let the slurry completely dry between coats, and bear in mind that this drying step will take longer than before because the slurry has more water than the slip you used to build up the line. These final coats will smooth out rough edges, fill in gaps and pinholes, and give the piece a clean, uniform look.

Make slurry by watering down PMC slip to the consistency of milk. Load up your brush and lightly flood the entire surface with a thin coat of slurry. Carefully get the brush into every recess. This is a delicate process—take care not to damage your raised lines. The object with this step is to smooth everything out, to give the piece what I like to call a clean even tone. I want the applied line to integrate into the base. In the end, the piece should look like a single work, not an object with slip drizzled on. When the piece looks right, set it aside to let everything dry completely.

When making a tall line, I allow the first layer or two to flow out and make a broad base. As the line grows, it is possible to control its lean depending on how each new layer is added.

PASTE AS A SCULPTURE MEDIUM

As I worked with this technique, I was pleasantly surprised to see how high I could build the lines. What started primarily as a drawing technique has evolved into a sensitive way to develop form. I'll use a bead to illustrate this extension of the process.

As before, the first step is to create a base form on which the viscosity painting will be done. In this case, I started with a kernel of Kix cereal covered with PMC. My preferred method is to reinforce the cereal with several coats of beeswax, a process that is made easier by skewering the Kix on a toothpick. Other waxes, like paraffin or candle wax can be used in a pinch, but the slip does not grip these as well. Also, beeswax softens at low temperatures, so even rolling it in your palms is enough to smooth out the surface. I make the bead by painting on seven to ten coats of slip, but it is also possible to cover the bead with a 2-card slab of PMC+ or PMC3.

When the bead is dry, draw the design on the surface with a pencil, then lay down a trail of PMC3 slip as described above. In my work, this first layer, and often the next, will be a little heavier than what I do when my objective is to make an ornamental line. This will give the form I am developing a wider and stronger base. As layers are added, the lines become thinner and narrower. After about the forth or fifth layer, I switch to a toothpick or needle tool instead of a brush to apply the paste. I cover the tip of the tool with a whisper of olive oil—dip, then wipe off almost all of it—and this seems to help the slip ease off the tip. Dip the tip of the tool into the slip jar to collect a droplet, then touch the tip of the drop to the existing line. As before, allow the needle to float a millimeter or two above the base, trailing a thin thread of slip along the top of the raised line. At this point, the scale is usually small, so I can make what appear to be significant additions with each pass. Remember, though, that it is still important to allow each layer to dry between coats.

This method is more sculptural because you can make the lines uneven, wavy, or varying in height. You can actually steer the tops of the lines by trailing the thread of slip along the outer edges of the wall that you have built up. To "bend" the walls, lay

PMC3 slip
1" high

the successive layer to the side of the previous application. This process can go on as long as you feel the form warrants it. On some of my sculpted beads, I have applied more then twenty layers (remember that mention of the obsessive illustrator?). I usually work on several pieces at once, so I can move through the series, allowing the pieces to dry as I work on others. As before, finish by applying a few coats of slurry to give the piece a clean and finished look. Allow to dry completely, then fire as recommended for the type of PMC you have used. For a bead, I set the work in a dish of vermiculite or on a pad of refractory wool to provide support. Like any other PMC work, pieces with viscosity painting are finished with burnishers, polishing papers, a brass brush, or tumbling. Patinas and/or Aura 22 can be used to make the contours more dramatic.

When I make beads, the first step is to coat the core with beeswax.

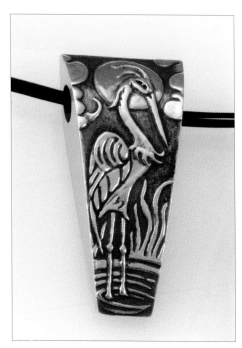

Crane Pendant
Fine silver, Aura 22
1³/₈" high

Noortje Meijerink

PMC on Ceramic

he desire to embellish vessels is almost as old as mankind. Especially in ceramics, form and decoration often merge into unique creations. Sometimes the purpose of the object determines both the shape and the decoration, while in other cases the decoration itself is the reason for making the pot. Every culture has its own master decorators—consider Chinese ware, the Mimbres Indians of North America, and the Dutch Delfts Blue among others.

BACKGROUND

Decoration on ceramics can take place at any stage of the process, from the making of the pot out of malleable clay, to patterning the glazed surface after the initial firing. Decoration can even mean combining clay with materials alien to the traditional potter. Combining two completely different materials is as exciting and challenging to me as a trip to an unknown country. Using PMC on ceramics is like clothing the pot, or even further, accessorizing the design already on the pot. In my work, I start by throwing porcelain clay on the potter's wheel to create a hollow form. When this is in the leather hard state, I cover it with black slip that I make myself. When that is dry, I polish the slip layer, which gives me the nicest

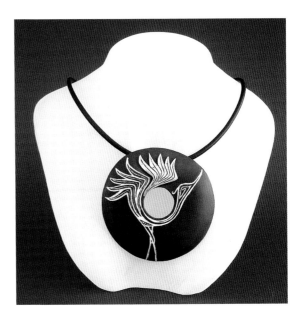

Rooster
Fine silver,
porcelain
3½" diameter

black surface after firing. The next step is to selectively scratch away the slip to reveal a design in white porcelain. These pots are fired only once, to 2300°F (1260°C). This is different from most coated pots, which are fired once without glaze (called the bisque firing) and a second time after the glaze or slip layer has been applied.

Before, the patterns I scratched onto my pots were solely geometric, and then I learned about PMC. Wouldn't it be fantastic to combine my own discipline with this new magic material? My geometric patterns changed into birds, and this allows the PMC element to play a role in embellishing the pots. My drawn birds, scratched out of earthen materials, are now adorned with silver wings!

This chapter will show how to combine PMC with ceramics and will hopefully encourage more potters to explore the rich possibilities of both materials. The pieces shown here use PMC3, but I see no reason why PMC+ would not work. I prefer PMC3 because it fuses faster than the other types.

KILNS

The techniques described here can be done in any type of electric kiln. The ideal case is to have a small programmable kiln for PMC and a larger ceramic kiln for pottery. Most people will probably have one or the other, depending on whether their primary work is in ceramics or metalwork. PMC artists working on a small scale can use their programmable kiln to fire small ceramic objects like beads or pendants, but they should know that firing above 2000° F (1100° C) pushes the kiln to its limits. If you intend to do a lot of work in ceramics, you should invest in a kiln made for the purpose.

Royal Wing
Fine silver,
porcelain
2½" high

PMC3 ON GLAZED WARE

All glazes used in ceramics are a form of glass. They are melted onto bisque-fired clays where they fuse to the surface of a pot and form a waterproof skin. We know from traditional enameling that glass and metals can be combined, so it is not surprising that the attachment of PMC to glaze is very good. However, there are important differences in the chemistry of various glazes. The aspect of most concern for this process is the temperature at which the glaze becomes fluid. Earthenware glazes, for instance, are fired in the range of 1650°F–2000°F (900°–1100°C). Stoneware glazes, including those made for porcelain are fired at 2100°F–2370°F (1150°–1300°C). Almost without exception, ceramic clays themselves must be fired at temperatures above the melting point of silver. This means that the ceramic work must be completely finished (both bisque and glaze firing) before the PMC elements are added.

In my case, even though the PMC parts come later, the silver elements are always in my mind as I design my pots. That is, I don't make a finished pot and then wonder where to apply a silver embellishment. Instead, I think through the design from the beginning, then make the ceramic element completely. Once the pot is out of the kiln and cooled—all traditional ceramic processes complete—then I turn my attention to the PMC components.

Especially for a complicated design, I often start by drawing on a piece of paper that I can cut out and lay over the pot. It is easier, faster, and a lot cheaper to work through variations this way than with the PMC. When I am satisfied with the form, I roll out a layer of PMC at a thickness of two cards, lay the paper pattern on top, and use a needle tool to cut out the shape. To compensate for the shrinkage of PMC, I cut at least two millimeters outside the paper pattern. For my designs, this approximation is sufficient, but if you do need to calculate, lay the paper design in a copier and enlarge by 115%.

Trace two or three millimeters outside the template to allow for shrinkage. Of course you can enlarge the drawing on a photocopier to be more accurate, but I find this method works fine for me.

Start with a paper pattern. This allows you to see the form directly on the pot. When you have the design you want, the paper also becomes a template for cutting out the PMC shape.

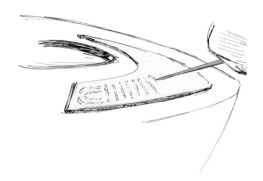

I like to work the wet clay directly on the pot, often inscribing my lines with a toothpick. Many decorative techniques can be used, including rubber stamps, appliqué, textured roller, and syringe.

When the clay is cut out, I lift the metal clay shape and drape it on the pot so it will follow the existing curves. Personally, I like to draw the lines and designs in the PMC with a toothpick or a blunt needle while it is still on the pot, but another possibility is to add texture to the original sheet before cutting it to shape. Any of the familiar ways of working PMC can be used at this point, including layering, carving, stamping, or water etching.

Once I am satisfied with the design, I let the PMC dry completely before taking it carefully off the pot. In my own work, I then make the PMC smooth, using 400 to 1200 grit polishing papers to refine the surfaces and smooth the edges.

In this example, I am securing the PMC onto a glazed surface. To secure the PMC to the pot, I paint a layer of PMC3 slip on the underside of the form. I don't paint right up to the edges because slip here might spill outward and ruin the clean edge of the metal piece. I usually leave about three millimeters of clearance from the edge. When this is done, I press the PMC form back into position on the pot and set it aside to dry.

Speedy
Fine silver, porcelain
2¾" wide

In this example, I am firing the PMC3 directly on the ceramic object, which has already been fired twice. To insure a grip, I paint PMC3 slip on the back of the piece, leaving several millimeters unpainted at the edges.

The pot, remember, has already been fired twice, once as bisque, and once for the glaze. Now we're heating to a lower temperature to sinter the PMC and simultaneously fuse the silver to the glaze. Fire at 1650°F (900°C) for 20 minutes. Unlike conventional PMC firing, though, in this situation, it is important to allow two or three hours for the kiln to reach temperature, and at least that long again for the work to cool. Unlike metal, ceramics cannot withstand rapid temperature changes. After this firing, the PMC will be fused with the glass surface of the pot, making a solid attachment.

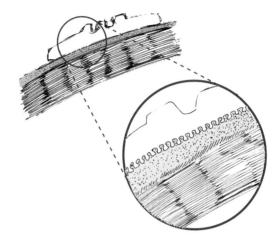

This stylized drawing shows how PMC elements are attached to glazed ceramics. The close-up on the right shows how the glaze layer has vitrified (become glassy) in its previous firing. At PMC temperatures, the glass softens enough to allow the silver to begin to mingle with it, creating a strong grip.

PMC3 ON UNGLAZED WARE

As I am throwing a pot on the wheel, an image of how the pot should look begins to form in my mind. In my work, I paint a layer of black slip onto the pot, then polish it smooth. During this process, I get a feel for the kind of bird I want to create. After the slip layer has dried, I scratch out the image, leaving the bird in white lines on a black background. The pot is then fired at the relatively high temperature (for PMC artists) of 2280°F (1250° C). In this process, the clay is vitrified, which means that the ceramic particles have fused together to form a non-porous mass. This dense structure means that it will be difficult for silver to grab onto the ceramic body. Like a smooth stone, there is nothing for the silver to grab onto. I want my wings to look airy, but I don't want them to fly off the surface! If I simply fire the PMC onto these pots, the absence of the glaze means the bond will not be very strong. I'm afraid that the silver part will come loose, so a different approach is needed.

fully fired = dense structure

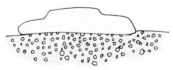

underfired = open structure

In properly fired ceramics, the unglazed clay fuses together to make a very dense structure. Ironically, this strong body makes it difficult for PMC elements to make a strong connection. The solution is to underfire the ceramic, leaving a structure that has microscopic spaces that allow the silver clay to gain purchase.

One solution would be to fire the PMC separate from the pot, bend it to match the contours, then attach it with epoxy or a similar strong adhesive. While this might work for some people, I think this method will always show in the final piece. There is a subtle interaction between the silver and ceramic components when the PMC shrinks directly on the pot. The effect is a natural look that is impossible to duplicate by bending parts after firing.

For this reason, I fire my PMC elements on the pots, then pull them loose (after the pots have cooled) and reattach them with epoxy. In effect, I am using the pot as a very specific firing support, knowing that it will yield a perfect match between the pot and the silver element.

Another possible way to fire PMC onto unglazed ceramic ware is to fire at higher temperatures than described above. This will create a better attachment between the parts, but working very near to the melting point of silver will remove most of the texture and detail on the PMC as well. Unglazed ware fired at earthenware temperatures is much more porous and will allow a much better attachment of the PMC. The melting point of silver is 1740°F (950°C), so you should not allow the kiln to rise above 1830°F (1000°C). Also, be aware that large kilns have different temperatures at different locations inside the chamber, depending on the location of the heat source. For instance, some electric kilns do not have coils in the floor or in the door, so those areas do not reach the same high temperatures as other places in the same kiln. Gas kilns reach their highest temperature near the burner, where the flame enters.

The third, and maybe the best way to fire PMC to unglazed ceramic, is to use glaze as a glue. A glaze with a melting point below 1750°F (950°C) will fuse with the silver and with the body of the pot. Paint a transparent glaze on the back of the PMC element, leaving about three millimeters from the edge clear. Do not use a colored glaze, because it will color the pot around the PMC piece. Fire up to the melting point of the glaze, reaching temperature slowly, and allowing several hours for the work to cool down. Because the metal is so near its melting point, it will be pulled by the glaze to mould to the contours of the pot.

Perhaps the best solution for attaching PMC to unglazed ceramics is to use a bit of glaze like a glue. Fire at the high end of the range recommended for the glaze to develop maximum strength.

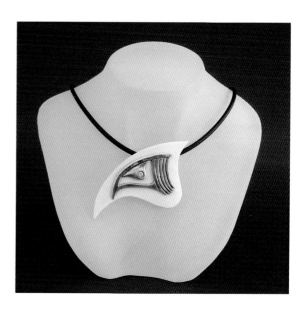

Eagle
Fine silver,
porcelain
3" wide

PMC3 SLIP ON GLAZED WARE

The best way to apply PMC slip to ceramic ware is with a synthetic paintbrush or a tool with a rubber tip. Apply at least three layers, allowing each coat to dry before adding a new layer. It is always better to apply several thin layers than a few thick ones. To achieve a bright shiny silver in the end, polish the dry PMC slip carefully with fine polishing paper before firing, even going up to something as fine as 8000 grit. If you wait to do all the burnishing after firing, you run the risk of creating a metallic film on the ceramic beside the decoration.

When the slip layer is dry and smooth, fire the pot at 1650°F (900°C) for at least 20 minutes, and again, allow the ceramic to cool slowly. Do not use a brass brush to shine the silver after firing. Instead I recommend abrasive sanding sponges and polishing papers to reach a high shine.

PMC3 SLIP ON UNGLAZED WARE

PMC slip attaches much better to unglazed ceramic surfaces than does PMC lump clay. The fluid slip is able to ooze into the clay, which creates a grip. By contrast, an ornament made of PMC in clay form will pull away from the ceramic base as it starts to shrink. With either method, there is an advantage to working on ceramic that was fired at a low temperature. The higher the ceramic is fired, the denser is the structure, leaving less purchase for the PMC embellishment. You will notice that PMC slip is much easier to apply to unglazed ware than it is on glazed ceramic; an indication of the way this porous surface soaks up the slip.

Use a brush, a swab, or any other drawing tool to paint PMC slip directly onto either glazed or unglazed ceramics. Three or more coats are usually needed.

PMC AND RAKU

Using Precious Metal Clay in a raku firing is as exciting as it is challenging. Those who are familiar with the raku process will know that the results are unpredictable—in fact, that's part of the pleasure. Be warned that raku is not a good fit for people who want to control a technique and take it to a predetermined result. For me, the idea of combining PMC with the gloss firing of raku arose from the fact that PMC matures at the same temperature as many raku glazes. Several popular raku glazes are fluid at 1650°F (900°C), a familiar number for those of us who work with PMC. This match of temperatures should allow the PMC to fuse with the glass component in the glaze as it is sintering, making the attachment of the PMC to the ceramic piece perfect.

Haiku
Fine silver,
porcelain
with raku glaze
3¼" diameter

The early steps of the process are the same as described above. Start by throwing or handbuilding the pot in any way you choose. Use the type of clay you are familiar with; this can be anything from special raku clay to porcelain. Bisque fire the piece at 1975°F (1080°C). Drape the PMC on the pot as described above. Allow the PMC to dry, then lift it off the pot and put it aside. Coat the bisqueware as usual with a raku glaze, either by brushing or dipping. Lay the dry PMC back on the glazed surface of the pot, but this time it is not necessary to add the layer of slip described earlier.

Most kilns are not large enough to fire all the pots in one time. This means you have to go through the process several times. Cooling the kiln completely between firings takes too much time. You allow the kiln to cool down to 400°C before loading it again. The raku clay can withstand temperature changes, so can PMC.

Allow the work to reach the maturation temperature of between 1650°–1740° F (900°–950° C). At this point, the PMC has fused into solid metal and the glaze has become fluid enough to bond to the underside of the attachment. In conventional raku firing, the work is pulled from the kiln at this point (using gloves, and tongs, of course) and set into a container filled with a combustible material like sawdust. It is usually allowed to set for a short time so the fluid glaze can harden enough that the sawdust won't leave marks. Because our goal is to have the glaze adhere the PMC to the pot, we skip this resting step and move the pot directly into the container of sawdust. Allow enough time to develop a good fire before clamping a lid on the container. This will stifle the fire and create a lot of smoke, which is what gives the raku glaze its particular color and iridescence. In conventional ceramic raku, the pot is hot enough to ignite the sawdust. When the scale shifts to small objects, it is possible that the heat will dissipate too quickly to set sawdust on fire. A traditional method to compensate for this is to set a stone or piece of ceramic in the kiln to heat up, and to drop this into the sawdust a minute before the pot to get things going. Another solution is to substitute tissue or paper towels as the combustible materials. Besides catching fire easily, these have the

Drape the PMC shape on the bisqued pot and allow it to dry there so it follows the contours of the vessel. When the clay is dry, lift it off, then paint the ceramic with raku glaze. Set the PMC element back into position, and keep the work horizontal so the PMC element doesn't fall off.

In typical raku fashion, bring the pot up to the temperature at which the glaze becomes fluid, then set it into a container of combustible material like leaves, sawdust, or pine needles. Allow the fire to get going well, then cover the container. At this point the PMC has sintered into the clay and become attached.

When the pot has cooled to the point where it can be held in the hands, remove it from the container and brush away the soot and ash that will have covered it.

advantage of avoiding marks made in the soft glaze by the sawdust. Avoid newspaper and magazine pages because the ink used there might give off environmentally unfriendly gases.

Leave the pot (now with silver attached) in the combustion container to cool down slowly. If you are like me, impatience and curiosity will urge you to take it out prematurely. Do not do it! Restrain yourself and leave your work in the reduction vessel for at least thirty minutes before taking it out. When you do pull it out, the pot will be covered with ash from the sawdust. Clean off the residue so you can admire the special raku effects. If you burnished the PMC element before firing, it will be a shiny silver as it comes from the kiln. I use an abrasive sanding sponge to remove the smoke residue and do some further polishing of the silver.

Peacock
Fine silver, porcelain, 3½" diameter

TROUBLESHOOTING

Now that the process is finished, it is possible to describe two possible problems that you might have encountered. It can sometimes happen that the silver element comes off, together with a chunk of the glaze. In this case, the glaze stuck well onto the underside of the metal (which we wanted) but came loose from the pot, which is something we did not want. A solution to this problem is to fire the bisqueware to a higher temperature, for instance, going to 2010°F (1100°C). This will result in a denser ceramic structure after firing, and the increased strength makes it less likely that the silver will peel off. However, when the pot has been fired at the higher temperature, you will notice that the crackling effect of the raku glazes does not occur. In conventional raku process, the lower temperature bisque firing leaves the clay porous, and this interacts with the raku glaze to create hundreds of hairline cracks as the glaze shrinks. Smoke enters through these cracks to color the lines, which creates the spider web effect. Firing high enough to strengthen the clay unfortunately comes at the cost of these appealing lines. I recommend a middle course, firing at

1975°F (1080°C) to get a compromise. This temperature will strengthen the ceramic vessel, but still permit enough shrinkage to generate some crackling. The number of lines is likely to be less than normal because of the need to put the ware into the reduction vessel immediately. To compensate for this, allow the fire to develop into a generous flame before clamping on the lid. Sometimes it works well to lift the pot so additional oxygen can come in beneath it and start the fire on the bottom of the vessel.

Q: Why do some parts of the PMC fuse into the ceramic and other parts don't?

A: When the PMC element has uneven thickness, you might notice that the thinner part attaches well, but the thicker part will curl upward. The more metal clay there is in a given area, the more apparent the shrinkage will be, so the thicker areas appear to shrink more. In this case, the PMC encounters resistance against the pot and shrinks into the "available" open space above the pot.

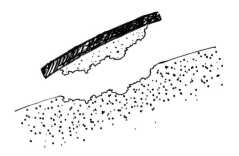

If the PMC component breaks off and pulls some of the ceramic with it, this tells us that the silver was well-fired, but the ceramic was underfired. The only way to fix this is with epoxy, but learn from this that you need to fire this clay hotter next time.

All PMC shrinks, but the effect is more pronounced on thicker pieces. In the upper example, the thick portion has pulled off the surface of the pot as it shrank. In the lower example, the thin portions are flexible enough that the tug of the glaze will pull them tight, and they will "steer" the shrinkage so it does not pull away.

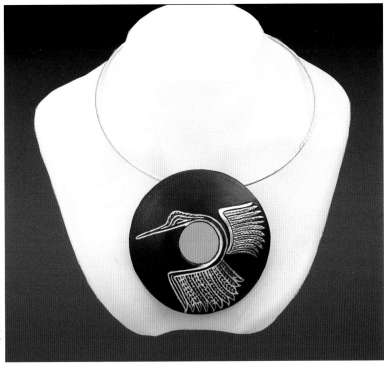

Bird
Fine silver,
porcelain
3½" diameter

Q: Why did the color of the glaze change?

A: Most glazes are colored with oxides, and these react with certain chemicals to create a specific color when heated to a certain temperature range. When PMC is heated, silver oxide is released as a vapor, and this will combine with the glaze to alter the color. Transparent or white glazes can turn yellow or (when you are lucky), into a beautiful light purple. Blue glazes sometimes change into green. In some cases, only the area around the PMC will undergo a color change, and other times the whole glazed pot will change color. This seems to depend on the type of glaze being used. I've also found that using a lot of different colored glazes in the same kiln can lead to a pleasant surprise.

Q: What accounts for the silver lines that I see around a PMC element?

A: Because of shrinkage, the finished silver part is smaller than it was before firing. If you paint slip across the entire underside, a residue of this slip will trail behind as the PMC shrinks. The slip layer has become stuck in the glaze, where it mingles and leaves a pale silver line. To prevent this, leave an unpainted rim of about 3–5 mm (about 1/8 inch) around the underside of the form.

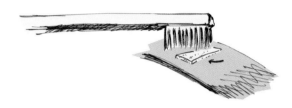

Brassbrushing after firing risks pushing a trace amount of silver into the ceramic, especially on an unglazed pot. To avoid this, polish with papers, which afford better control.

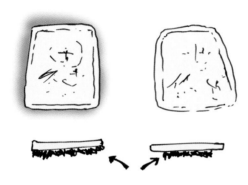

When gluing parts with either slip or glaze, don't paint either all the way to the edges. When the PMC shrinks, this will ooze outward and show on the finished pot. Instead, leave two or three millimeters unpainted around the edge.

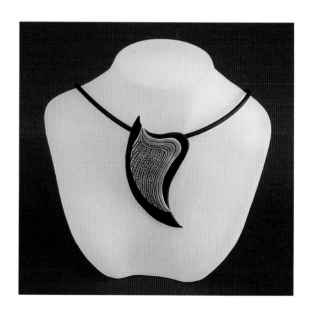

Wing Pendant
Fine silver, porcelain
4¼" high

Q: After finishing, I see a faint metal film on the pot around the silver element. Where did this come from?

A: The ghost image is created, usually by accident, when burnishing the PMC after all the firing is complete. You'll notice that it is especially obvious on unglazed ceramic, which makes sense. The clay body is porous, and easily picks up silver particles that are pressed into it during burnishing. To avoid this problem, polish very carefully. Use as small a brass brush as possible and, when using polishing papers, fold them into small squares so you can avoid contact with the pot. I find I have the most control (and therefore get the best results) with a burnishing tool.

Q: What happens if the PMC melts?

A: If the temperature in the kiln goes above the melting point of silver, two things can happen. When you use a glaze that melts just above the melting point of silver, say around 1740°–1830°F (950°–1000°C), the silver starts to melt, enters a semi-solid, slushy state, and blends into the glaze. This makes a glass/metal hybrid material. When this happens on a vertical surface (like the side of a pot) the PMC will drip down like tears. When the melting point of the glaze is higher than 1830°F (1000°C) and you actually are heating up to this temperature, the PMC will melt and form spherical droplets on top of the glaze. PMC slip acts the same way when heated over 1740°F (950°C).

When it is hot enough, glaze is fluid enough to drip under the pull of gravity. If there is PMC slip in the glaze, it will mingle in the glaze and also drip down a vertical surface.

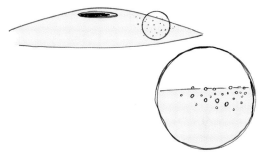

If PMC is heated above its melting point, the silver will separate into tiny bits that will pull themselves into very small spheres that will be locked in the glaze layer. This can be an interesting effect, but it is difficult to control.

Kelly Russell

Using Stencils with PMC

In a relatively short time, artists around the world have pushed past the immediate uses of Precious Metal Clay to explore methods that reach beyond not only the techniques, but the effects associated with traditional metalworking. The techniques described here take advantage of the semi-liquid state of thick slip to develop patterns through the use of stencils. As fascinating as the technique is in its elemental form, it is in the variations and potential uses of the resulting metal forms that the mind is truly carried away.

STENCILS WITH PMC

When I was younger, my family lived for a few years in Morocco. We would go on family outings to see the Roman ruins in Volubius, near Tangiers, and into the marketplaces of Fez and Rabat. I was always amazed at the textures and patterns on the buildings, the arches, and in the gardens. The mosaics at Volubius are something to see, and the Botanical Gardens there are unbelievable. I have always had a passion for antiqued and weather-worn architecture, and I think it traces back to that time of my life. I now try to replicate these surfaces and textures on my beads.

I remember experimenting at my workbench one day in an effort to layer PMC in such a way that it looked carved, like the stonework I had seen in Morocco and Spain. And more than just carved, I wanted a look that appeared rough and rich in the same way as the ancient walls that had been abraded by wind and sand for centuries. From the start, PMC appealed to me because of the wealth of textures it invites. I am more interested in achieving a sense of the passage of time than in a highly refined finish. In my quest to find a way to create that look on a miniature scale, I came up with the techniques described here.

Many commercial stencils are made to add decorative trim to walls, which makes them too large for jewelry scale work. Also, the designs may not fit with your aesthetics.

When planning stencils, it is important to plan ahead. If you are not careful, interior elements like the center of this letter "O" will disappear. Oops!

Plan bridges into the design to hold center pieces in place. This is illustrated in familiar stencil lettering.

STENCILS

The building block of this process is a stencil—a sheet of resilient material with a design cut out in the form of separate holes. Stencils come in two types of materials, and from two very different sources.

The best stencils are made of thin brass. They have the advantage of being somewhat rigid, and being tough enough to stand up to hundreds of uses. The alternative is plastic, and while these can last a long time, they are just not as strong. Also, metal stencils can accommodate smaller openings, including thin lines, so they open more design options.

The other big difference is between commercial stencils and those you make yourself. Commercial stencils can be lovely—laser-cut brass or plastic sheets that are precise and mechanically perfect. At the same time, because they are manufactured, you will be using stencils that are available to other artists too. Efforts to be unique start with a built-in challenge when you're using the same tools as others. Also, I find that commercial stencils don't always provide the motifs I want. For those reasons, and also just for the pleasure of the craft, it is great to be able to make your own.

The first step is to create a design or locate a pattern you can use. There are books with copyright-free patterns from almost every era, from Anasazi to Art Deco. People with computer skills might like to manipulate photos, or develop patterns from geometric sources. Whether you are using a computer, a photocopier, or your own two hands, a stencil has specific requirements. Think of the letter "O" and what will happen when you cut it out to make a stencil. That's right—unless you take special steps, the center of the "O" will fall out and you'll be left with a large dot. A look at some letters rendered for stencils show not only the challenge, but some possible solutions.

A stencil must avoid patterns that create large flaps of stencil material that can lift up, and designs that call for sharp points, because they are also likely to lift up. It is not that these patterns cannot be made as stencils, but it is important to anticipate problems and design around them. Draw connectors where they are needed, rather than tell yourself to build them in as you cut out the stencil. Trust me on this; you'll have other things on your mind while you're cutting.

Plastic stencils can be cut in almost any plastic sheet, but 5 mil Mylar is probably the best choice. Acetate is a similar plastic sheet, but it is prone to tearing, and you'll want this stencil to be around for a while. Thinner Mylar is easier to cut, but the relief created is rather timid. I have also tried a much thicker plastic sold expressly for this purpose, but it is quite thick for work on a jewelry scale.

Set the plastic sheet over the drawing and trace it with a fine permanent marker. Some Mylar is made for this purpose, but for other sheets, you might need to lightly sand the sheet to create a tooth that will hold the ink. I draw inside the line so that if I make a mistake I can fix the edge and still retain correct proportions. Besides just being necessary, I find that this step is helpful because it makes me think through just how the stencil will work. When the drawing is transferred to the sheet, set it onto a piece of mat board or a self-healing cutting board and cut out the openings. I use both a straight and a swiveling X-Acto blade. The swivel takes some practice to control, but it is great for tight curves and small circles. Mylar is cheap, so don't be shy about using a sheet to practice before you start on your design.

Avoid long, skinny pieces of stencil, like the area shown by the arrow. This will lift up in use, ruining the design. The figure on the right shows a variation that does not have any flimsy points.

Trace the pattern onto the plastic with a permanent marker. If using metal, transfer or print onto adhesive (label) paper and apply it to a sheet of 24 gauge brass. Cut through paper and metal together, then peel the paper off.

Garden Lock
Fine silver, 24k gold, sterling, enamel, opals
1" by 1½"

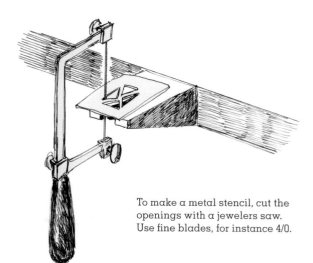

To make a metal stencil, cut the openings with a jewelers saw. Use fine blades, for instance 4/0.

For a thicker and almost unbreakable stencil, use a jewelers saw to pierce a piece of brass that is 22 or 24 gauge (0.6–0.5 mm or 0.025–0.020"). Draw or print the image onto adhesive paper, and stick this onto the metal. Drill a small hole in each opening, and pierce with a fine sawblade such as 4/0 or finer. For both plastic and metal, I suggest working from the center out; this provides the most structural strength as you are working. When the sawing is complete, rub both sides of the metal aggressively with sandpaper, steel wool, or powdered pumice to remove all burs and roughness.

Broken
Fine silver
1¼" by 1¼"

PREPARATION

Perhaps the most important discovery of my experimentation is the fact that this process requires that you work on dry metal clay. Before you can stencil, you need to create what we might think of as a canvas. In my work, this is typically a freeform panel of PMC rolled to a modest thickness of two cards. I usually have a general idea of the size and shape piece of clay I need for the project, but it is not my style to work out a specific pattern in advance. Of course, that's just me. This process works equally well on all types of PMC, though I find I usually use PMC+ or Original PMC. It is important to use a single type throughout the piece; the base and the slip should be the same material.

The other ingredient is PMC slip, and this must be considerably thicker than the factory-made material. Either make your own from scratch, or add sandings from dry PMC to the commercial material to thicken it. How thick? Even a spoon can hold itself upright in my jar

of slip. The texture resembles thick frosting, or the joint compound used to fill bumps in sheetrock. It's thick.

To provide proper release, coat the stencil generously with olive oil. I do not use balm for this because it might clog up fine holes and thin lines.

Commercial slip is too thin for this process. Thicken it by adding PMC dust made by sanding dry pieces of PMC. It should be thick enough that a spoon will stand upright.

Wedding Ring
Fine silver
1¾" diameter

USING THE STENCIL

Press the stencil firmly on the dry panel and spoon a generous blob of slip on the solid area of the stencil, outside the pattern. Press the stencil down firmly, and use a palette knife to smear the soft clay across the stencil. I find it best if I can accomplish this in a single fluid movement. It's OK to move the knife back and forth, as long as the stencil itself doesn't move.

When I first developed this technique, I thought it would be best to allow the slip to harden before removing the stencil. That's a great idea, especially if you want lots of tiny shattered pieces. In fact, it turns out that it works best to lift the stencil off the clay (plastic) or the clay off the stencil (metal) right away. Obviously you want to avoid smearing the image by dragging the stencil sideways, but other than that, there is nothing special in the process. Pull the stencil away and set the work aside to dry.

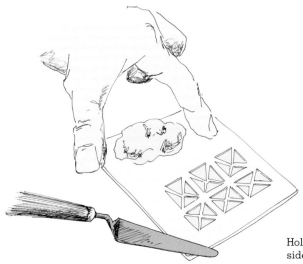

Hold the stencil firmly so it can't slide sideways. Swipe a mound of slip across the stencil with a flexible tool like a palette knife, then lift the stencil off.

VARIABLES

As simple as this technique is, there are options at every turn. Perhaps because the process is so simple, even small variations seem to yield significant changes. For some, this might be an invitation to an ulcer, but for me, this is where the fun begins. Here are a few variables to get you started.

• *Double Up*

Lay down a layer of slip as described, then repeat the process a second time with the same stencil. Even if you try to match up the layers perfectly, you'll probably find a bit of irregularity around the edges. And of course the first layer is a bit smaller because of shrinkage as it dries.

Magic Carpet
Fine silver,
colored pencil
1" by 2¼"

Faded Garden
Fine silver, colored pencil
1¼" by 1" by 1"

• *Double Up with a Sag*

Squeeze a second layer through a stencil over a dry first layer, but in this case, use conventional thin slip. This will flow over the edges of the initial pattern, making a softer, goopier look.

• *Stenciling on Air*

Not really, but this is the effect that I get when I selectively crumble the panel away from beneath the stenciled pattern at the edges. After the whole piece is dry, I nibble away at the edges with my fingernails, breaking off small pieces of the relatively thin panel (2 cards). Often I find that pieces of the applied layer overhang the broken area, and to me this looks like broken stonework.

• *Bright Highlights*

This variation requires a generous height in the stenciled pattern, so I recommend two applications. Before firing, rub a fine sanding stick over the surface to smooth the areas that are raised. Repeat the process after firing, then follow up with a burnisher to bring those areas to a bright shine. This will contrast dramatically with the rough textured recesses.

• *Stucco Over*

This one takes some nerve, but I like the result. Once you've created your pattern and allowed it to dry, smear some fresh slip directly over the pattern, as if to conceal it. This reminds me of the layers often seen in architecture, where the covering layer of one generation peels away to reveal a structure beneath.

Ivory Lace
Fine silver,
spray paint,
Mabe pearl
1¾" diameter

FINISHING

As if there weren't enough options on the table already, let me introduce a few more. The variations above are only a few of the dozens that remain to be tried. Shifting sequence, viscosity, tools, and types of clay can yield exciting possibilities all by themselves. And then there is finishing.

Of course one possibility is to simply polish a fired stencil piece with a brass brush or by tumbling. Personally, I prefer the drama that comes with patina, so I usually use liver of sulfur to add color to my pieces. Other options for color include enamel, resins, colored pencil, polymer clay, and paint. In every case, these can be used with boldness that covers much of the surface, or a subtlety that only hints at its hues. In the case of paints, pastels, and patinas, the usual method is to apply a full coat, then selectively remove color to create the desired effect. Use steel wool, polishing papers, or turpentine, depending on the material.

CONCLUSION

If I had to summarize my aesthetic in a few words, they would be these: If it works, it works. I have been lucky enough to stumble into a vocabulary and palette that works for me. It is not yours, but perhaps these techniques will help you find your own look. One thing is for sure—getting there is half the fun.

Floral Fragment
Fine silver, colored pencil
¾" by 1¾"

Tautology
Effetre, sodalime, & dichroic glass,
fine silver, sterling
bead diameters: ¾" high

Barbara Becker Simon

Lampworking and PMC

ne of the intriguing aspects of Precious Metal Clay is the way it has attracted artists whose primary medium is polymer clay, glass, ceramics, or other crafts. Every once in a while, a person like Barbara Becker Simon comes along who has training and experience in several fields. In her case, a background in traditional metal-smithing gave over to years of working with polymer clay before sliding into lampworking glass.

As rich as each of these fields is, the possibilities that arise when media are combined is extraordinary. In this article, Barbara describes several ways to build lampworked glass beads over a fine silver core. The techniques described here assume an understanding of lampworking techniques—a full description is outside the scope of this book. When the process being described requires specific information though, you'll find all the particulars here. Lampworkers will be able, after reading this, to get right to work. Others will very likely have a strong desire to learn about lampworking…

BACKGROUND

My "other life" (as I like to characterize it to my PMC friends), is creating lampworked glass beads. I began practicing this enticing art form in 1996, one year before learning the joys of PMC. Is it any mystery that I wanted to combine the two media? The obvious combination is to make glass beads and string them along with PMC beads and clasps that are complementary in design. In that case, the silver and glass elements are made separately and brought together only in the final assembly. That version of combining glass and PMC works great, and I've made a lot of pieces that way, but I wanted something more.

In 2002, I tried an experiment. I made a PMC core in the shape of a spool, fired it, tumbled it, then built a hollow glass bead around it using traditional lampworking techniques. Now this was something new—a single piece that combined the shine and value of silver with the luster and color of glass. Much to my delight, it worked. Since then, I've made dozens more beads like this, experimenting each time to test new configurations.

Because glass and metal expand and contract at different rates, I wondered if the glass would eventually crack or pop off the PMC. I am happy to report that the original bead, made in 2002, is still in tact. I conclude that fine silver and most soda lime glass are compatible and bear further exploration. I have found that the transparent light purple Effetre/Moretti color is not compatible. A bead made with this glass looked fine when first made, but cracked later. I have experimented with Bullseye and borosilicate glass and found them to be equally usable.

PMC Spool Beads
Effetre and Bullseye soda
lime glass.
Largest bead is 1³/₈" high

MAKING A HOLLOW BEAD ON A PMC SPOOL

The first step is to make a PMC structure that
will be the core of the final bead. Any version of PMC can be used and I generally
work with all of them with no real preference.
Begin by making a tube of PMC, for instance
over a drinking straw. This will yield a tube
with an inner diameter large enough to fit
around a ³/₃₂" or ¹/₈" bead mandrel after firing.
The length of the tube depends on the design
of the bead and your skill level as a bead-
maker. A hollow bead requires advanced
lampworking skills, so, unless you are an advanced glass artist, make the tube less than
one inch long. Once you've got the hang of
the technique, or if you are willing to skip the
hollow part and build the glass directly on the
PMC spool, the length can be longer.

Roll out PMC to a thickness of two cards,
and wrap this around the straw to make a
tube. Make sure that the seam is well connected. I like to build up caps on the end
of the bead. These give the bead a more
finished appearance, provide more area to
decorate, and provide increased support for
the glass structure. Build the ends in any of
the familiar ways we work with PMC. Roll
out a sheet that is three cards thick, and cut
a hole with the same size straw that you
used for the tube. Wiggle the straw a little to
enlarge the hole, then create the shape of the
outer pieces. Disks or rectangles are a good
choice—stay away from irregular shapes

Make a spool-shaped core from any version of PMC.
I often start by wrapping a rectangle of rolled PMC
around a drinking straw. I use clay rolled to two cards
thick for the tube and three cards for the end caps.

Make end caps of the same type of PMC as the tube.
These can be plain or textured. Construction, firing, and
finishing are just like any other PMC object.

because they are difficult to work around when you start to build with hot glass. Attach the caps to the PMC tube securely with thick slip. Let this dry before decorating for ease of handling.

I try to relate the decoration of the shaft and the end caps. Resist the temptation to put a high relief on the shaft because the glass may touch these silver parts as you are making the hollow bead and this may cause the bead to collapse.

Allow the spool to dry and then refine if needed with sandpaper or carving tools. Up to this point, this is all standard PMC practice. Fire the PMC at the recommended temperature. Note: spools made of Original PMC are more likely to sag than the denser versions, PMC+ and PMC3. To compensate for this, roll a bit of paper clay (the volcanic ash product) into a rod a little less than the diameter of the hole and a little longer than the spool. Allow it to dry, then insert it into the opening of the spool to support it during firing.

PMC and PMC3 don't need to be fired at 1650° F and will not be subject to the sagging effect of heat and gravity. As a precaution, though, all types of clay should be supported. A small stainless steel bowl (kitchen stores are a good resource) filled with vermiculite is good for supporting the spool during firing.

After firing, finish the spool, again using any of the usual methods familiar to PMC artists. I recommend a mirror finish, which takes full advantage of the reflective nature of silver. Or to say it another way, why go to the expense and effort of making a silver core if it's not going to add the Bling? The lampworking process will work equally well on matte PMC, but in my opinion, the effect is less

To make the most of the effect, decorate the basic spool, for instance with PMC syringe.

Allow the PMC spools to dry completely then fire them according to any of the recommended firing schedules. I usually set the work into a bowl of vermiculite to support the forms in the kiln.

Dip a steel mandrel into bead release, then slide the PMC spool onto the mandrel. When the release dries, it will cement the silver core temporarily to the mandrel. When the bead is complete, the release will be broken away and the bead will slip off the mandrel.

than exciting. Remember that even when the surface is polished, we'll be seeing it through a layer of glass, so whatever shine you have to start with will be slightly reduced. All the more reason, I think, to get as bright a shine as you can on the silver before moving into the glasswork. I usually use a tumbler and stainless steel media.

Once it is polished, mount the spool onto a bead mandrel so it can be manipulated during the lampworking process. These stainless steel rods are usually either $3/32$" or $1/8$" in diameter and about 10" long. The ideal arrangement is that the hole in the silver spool is just slightly larger than the mandrel, which will allow for a layer of bead release coating. This coating is a commercial product that secures the bead while working, but allows it to come free later. Dip the mandrel in your preferred bead release, making sure that it is dipped to a depth longer than the spool. While the bead release is still wet, slide the spool onto the mandrel. Bead release will ooze out the leading edge, which is OK. This will be easily removed after the bead is annealed. Set the mandrel-with-spool aside to dry, with the mandrel laying horizontally.

The ends of the PMC spool offer an opportunity to create patterns that will coordinate with the glass work.

PMC Spool Bead
Effetre soda lime glass
¾" diameter

CHOOSING WHICH GLASS TO USE

The choice of glass is a personal preference, but here are some recommendations. Either borosilicate or soda lime glass will work when wrapping a silver core. A word of caution about using borosilicate glass with the PMC spools: The temperatures required to melt boro are very close to the melting point of fine silver. If you aren't watchful of your flame as you work, the PMC could start to melt. If you have decorated the spool—that is, if there is detail that you want to be easily seen—choose a very light transparent color so the ornamentation can be seen through the glass. Transparent cobalt, teal, red, and the like are too dark to allow the PMC shaft to be seen. Pale aqua, mint green, pale blue are better choices. Clear or colorless transparent soda lime glass sometimes turns an amber color when it comes into contact with silver. If you are willing to accept the random nature of this coloration, that's also a good choice.

This bead is made of borosilicate glass, which has working temperatures very near the melting point of PMC. In this sample, the end of the spool was accidentally melted in the process of making the bead.

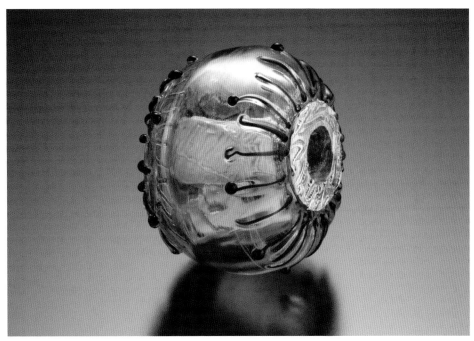

PMC Spool Bead
Effetre soda
lime glass
1" diameter

MAKING A HOLLOW BEAD

To make a hollow bead on the PMC spool, gently warm the bead release and the PMC, being careful not to melt the silver. Start by wrapping the first gathers at each inside end where shaft meets end cap. From there on, build successive gathers alternately on each end. Start by working perpendicular to the spool, laying the glass up against the end caps to make a snug fit. As the height of the glass reaches above the caps, set each successive gather slightly to the inside edge of the former layer until they meet in the middle. Be careful to melt each succeeding gather into the previous one. Even the tiniest pinhole will cause the bead to collapse.

Continue adding rings of glass in the sequence shown, keeping the glass hot enough that each layer fuses into the previous one. Warm air inside the closed form will expand slightly, pushing the glass into a pleasantly rounded form.

If the first step is to get the glass more or less where you want it, the second step is to smooth it and create the desired form. Once you have gathered all the glass onto the spool, slowly and patiently turn the bead in the flame to smooth out the gather lines and "puff up" the hollow. The position of the bead in the flame should be as shown here—only the equator of the bead should touch the edge of the flame, not the entire bead.

At this point, other embellishments may be added to the glass bead such as stringers or dots. Remember, though, that you have a sparkling PMC spool shaft under the glass and limit your decoration to only what will contribute to the bead and not conflict or camouflage the silver. My advice is to keep it simple.

Roll the bead against the underside of the flame to smooth the surface and refine the shape. Be careful to use only the edge of the flame so the silver element does not melt.

If your hollow bead doesn't "cooperate," (i.e., if it collapses), you have two choices in how to proceed. You can accept it as a partially hollow bead or plunge it into a can of water while it is still hot. This will shatter the glass and release the spool from the mandrel. To reuse the spool, clean off any remaining glass, retumble to restore the finish, and remount the piece on a mandrel for another try.

Once the glass bead is finished, place the entire mandrel, PMC, glass and all in a bead kiln for annealing. This process is an important part of any work with hot glass because it allows stresses to be reduced. Without proper annealing, glass objects are like time bombs, certain to eventually crack or shatter. For this bead, follow the normal annealing schedule for the glass that was used. Do not rush the cooling of this bead. The phases of annealing known as the slow cooling phase and the equilibrium phase might even be extended a little in respect to the metal in this bead; the longer the dwell time on the strain point of your glass, the better. I usually add an additional 30 minutes to these phases of the annealing procedure. By the way, if there are "normal" (a.k.a. non-PMC beads) in the kiln, this extension of time won't harm them.

After annealing, remove the bead from the mandrel and finish the exposed PMC of the end caps. The bead can be put in the tumbler, but be sure to thread a pipe cleaner through the hole to prevent steel shot from wedging itself in the opening. Brassbrushing, patinas or any other form of finishing can be done without damaging the glass.

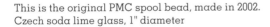

Continue adding rings of glass in the sequence shown, keeping the glass hot enough that each layer fuses into the previous one. Warm air inside the closed form will expand slightly, pushing the glass into a pleasantly rounded form.

This is the original PMC spool bead, made in 2002. Czech soda lime glass, 1" diameter

This clear hollow bead allows texture on the spool to show through. In this example I have used spheres on the shaft, the endcaps, and in the glass.

VARIATIONS

MAKING A SOLID BEAD

These are actually a little easier than the hollow bead just described, so if you are a novice lampworker, you might want to start here. Make a spool shape as described above, but don't bother to decorate the shaft because the glass will be built directly onto the PMC and this portion won't show much. If you are using transparent glass, tumble the spool to a mirror finish so some reflection can come through. If you are going to use opaque or translucent glass, don't waste the time and effort to polish the shaft because it won't show. Either way, the end caps will be finished.

It is possible to make solid beads on PMC spools, and in fact this is a good place to start. Bullseye soda lime glass, ¾" diameter.

TWO ENDCAPS ON A MANDREL

In this variation, you make two separate endcaps and allow the glass bead to connect them. This is a little trickier than the hollow bead as described above, but it saves on PMC and allows you to adjust the size of the bead after you see how the silver turns out. The process is as above.

Make two endcaps in any version of PMC, fire and finish as usual. Attach them about an inch apart on a mandrel that was just coated with bead release. Let the bead release dry, then look closely at the area on the inside of each cap. If there is any excess release here, clean it away now while it is easy to reach. This variation creates "built in" end caps that are connected only by the glass that bridges the two silver pieces. A hollow or a solid bead can be built on these two end caps.

In this variation, the end caps are not connected by a metal tube. Instead, the glass will hold the silver parts in place when the bead is completed. This style is especially good for long beads, where the cost or weight of the silver might be prohibitive.

CENTRAL DISK

In this variation, a silver disk at the center of the spool will create a silver line in the center of the bead. Start by making a flat disk that is three or four cards thick, and mount it centrally on a PMC tube. The tube can have endcaps as shown, or you can do without them. As before, fire the PMC, give it a shiny finish, and slide it onto a mandrel that has just been dipped into bead release. Allow this to dry so the release cements the silver core firmly into place. You can build either a solid or a hollow bead on this armature. Though the result is a single bead, in reality you are building two half-beads, one on each side of the central wall.

It is also possible to make a bead with a silver element in the center, for instance at the equator like this. The design work is done in the PMC—the lampwork is the same as for the other beads described here.

PMC Spool Bead with Center Disk
Soda lime glass
1¼" diameter

In this example, solid glass is wrapped around a silver core made by wrapping a PMC rod aound a PMC tube.

PMC Spool Bead, soda lime glass
$1^1/8$" long, ½" diameter

SNAKE BEAD

For this variation, start with a PMC tube, for instance, by wrapping a rolled sheet around a drinking straw. Roll out a rod of PMC about ⅛" in diameter and wind this around the tube, securing it with water or slip as needed to insure a secure joint. You can add endcaps or not. Allow this to dry, then fire it using any of the usual PMC methods. As before, refine and finish the form, typically to create a high polish. Secure onto a mandrel, and after drying, warm the silver in the lampworking flame. Attach a gather of glass and wrap it around the bead so that the glass lays into the space between the silver wraps. If you have no PMC end caps, make end caps by layering a gather or two of glass on the ends.

A variation on this variation is to omit the internal silver tube. Wrap the PMC rod around a drinking straw, allow to dry, then fire and tumble. Slide the silver coil onto a mandrel with bead release and allow it to dry. Carefully clean off any bead release that has gotten onto the silver, and wrap with hot glass as above.

Start with a tube of PMC made over a drinking straw, then wrap a PMC rod around it in a spiral. Use water or slip to insure a tight fit. End caps can be added if desired. Fire and polish as usual, then wrap a thread of hot glass between the silver coils.

In this example there is no tube. Instead, the glass is formed directly over a mandrel coated with release.

PMC Snake Bead
Effetre soda lime glass
1³/₈ by ½" diameter

This bead is like the last one except that it is not built on a tube. Make a PMC spiral on a straw or similar burnable core, fire, and finish. Slide this onto a mandrel prepared with bead release and wrap with glass. After annealing, break the release and remove the bead.

ENAMEL/PMC HYBRID ON SPOOL

Because of the clay-like nature of PMC, it is possible to knead powdered enamels into the clay to create a metal/clay hybrid. This enticing material could be used in any of the variations described here, which makes it possible to introduce color not only in the glass, but in the metal element as well.

ADDING BITS OF GLASS TO THE SHAFT

Create a PMC spool with a lightly textured shaft. Fire, tumble, and mount on a mandrel with bead release. Before building the hollow bead, put small dots of glass directly on the shaft using a contrasting color of glass either transparent or opaque.

PMC Spool Bead
Effetre soda lime glass.
¾" diameter

This bead has hybrid PMC/enamel elements on the shaft and the ends of the spool.

PMC Spool Bead
Enamel, Effetre soda lime glass
¾" diameter

In this hollow bead I have attached glass spheres to the shaft of the core.

CeCe Wire

Water Etching

Traditional metal etching uses strong acids to dissolve the surface of a metal. Control is achieved by painting an acid-proof resist such as paint or a tarry substance called asphaltum on those areas that are intended to remain at their original height. Etching produces rich effects, and has been used for centuries, but it has always involved dangerous chemicals and tedious labor. The technique I describe here replaces asphaltum with wax and acid with water—it is hard to imagine a more dramatic reversal, from slow and dangerous to quick and safe. This PMC stuff is amazing!

BACKGROUND

When I first started working with Precious Metal Clay, I investigated pottery techniques because PMC is so similar to fine porcelain. My research into techniques used by ceramic artists led me to water etching, a technique that uses the water solubility of PMC but achieves the look of acid etching in metal. I was first introduced to the wonders of water etching by Professor Emeritus Richard Luster in his home studio in Greeley, Colorado. He has been using the technique for many years as surface decoration on his wheel-thrown porcelain vessels to acquire beautifully subtle surfaces that are further enhanced by the use of transparent glazes.

This technique has its origins in a process used by potters to prevent their glazed ceramic ware from sticking to kiln shelves during firing. If the glaze covered the pots completely, those areas that rest on the shelf will fuse when the glaze melts. To prevent this, it is necessary to leave certain areas unpainted. Selectively avoiding certain areas is difficult, especially when applying glaze by dipping the pot into a vat, so a wax resist method was invented. Potters regularly apply a layer of water-soluble wax to the base of their pieces before applying glaze. When the piece is fired in a kiln, the wax burns away in the early stages of the glaze firing cycle to reveal the bisqued clay body. This unglazed section is what sits on the kiln shelf during the glaze firing.

In the water etching technique, wax resist is used in a decorative manner rather than this practical way. The wax is applied to specific areas of unfired porcelain. This opaque white liquid wax has the consistency of milk, and can be applied with a brush, a sponge, or almost any other painting tool. The wax is allowed to dry overnight—it is critical that it is fully set. Once the wax is dry, a damp sponge is used to wipe away successive layers of exposed clay, thus "etching" away the background.

My research shows that all formulas of PMC will work with this technique. My preference is PMC+ because it yields a crisper edge. Water etching on Original PMC and PMC3 will result in the edges of the design becoming somewhat fuzzy during the wiping stage.

The PMC pieces must be completely dry before applying resist. Allow them to dry naturally, or speed up the process with a mug warmer.

PROCESS

By definition, water etching is a process of removal, so it makes sense to start with a thick slab. Of course this will depend on the intended design—the technique offers a range from subtle undulations to geologic drama—and you should have your goals in mind from the outset. I typically work on PMC+ slabs that are between three and eight cards thick (2 - 4mm).

In some designs, I start by etching a panel that is then cut to shape and used in the construction of a finished piece, as in the enameled pendant on this page. In other cases, it makes sense to construct the piece first, then do the water etching. Imagine a box, for instance, in which you want a pattern that winds unbroken around the form. It makes the most sense to assemble the box first, then to etch; the box on page 111 is an example. That said, it is easiest to work on a flat surface, so that method might be the best one for your first attempt.

The piece needs to dry thoroughly before you apply resist. Drying can be hastened by using gentle heat, a dehydrator, or moving air, for instance, from a hair dryer or furnace vent. I typically set my PMC+ panel on a coffee mug warmer to speed up the drying process. If the clay starts to warp, I press it down with a metal spatula and hold it for a few seconds until it sets.

Ode to Jasper Johns Fine silver, sterling, pink sapphire, enamel. 2¼" high

RESISTS

The original method, as I learned it, depended on water-soluble wax, which is readily available from pottery supply houses. There are several brands, and they all seem to be similar in consistency, cost, and drying time. As I worked with the technique, I came to realize that because our needs are different than those of a potter, other resist options were worth trying. The resist needs to be easy to apply, it needs to adhere to the dry PMC well, and it must be waterproof. In the following chart, I have listed my experiences to date, but it is worth noting that there are many other materials that merit experimentation.

Comparison of Resists

	Advantages	*Disadvantages*
Potters Wax Resist	• Available in pint size • Inexpensive and will last forever if working jewelry scale • Initially holds up well to repeated damp wiping • Good for three-dimensional objects like beads	• Takes a long time to dry, best to let sit overnight • Wax creates smoke during firing • Because it is water-soluble, it will wash away with too much wiping
Nail Polish	• Available at drug stores and discount stores • Inexpensive • Tenacious and definitely waterproof	• Noxious fumes during burn-out and firing • Leaves a faint surface texture after firing • Some brands & colors leave discoloration on the silver
Masking Tape	• Widely available • Inexpensive • Good for crisp lines (cut tape with scissors)	• Will not stand up to aggressive rubbing • Not good for rounded surfaces • Not good for painterly effects
Car Detailing Tape (electrical tape is similar)	• Will hold up to aggressive wiping • Can achieve crisp sharp lined and bold graphic designs	• Must be purchased at a specialty car detailing shop • Limited to straight designs • Not for rounded surfaces
Floor & Porch Paint	• Works exceedingly well as a resist	• Must be purchased in large quantities • Noxious fumes released during firing

APPLICATION OF RESISTS

I normally use a sumi brush to paint gestural lines and patterns, but the range of possibilities for applying the resist is huge. Some liquid resists are thicker than others, and your choice of which to use will take this into account. Some patterns might require delicate painting with a fine-tipped watercolor paintbrush. Other patterns could be as loose as dabbing with a sponge or a crumbled piece of paper to create an interesting surface. I can also imagine the use of stencils, silkscreens, and rubber stamps. Further, we should take advantage of the various viscosities of the resists. Just as painters achieve exciting effects by allowing paint to drip or splatter, we can choose what we paint, what we paint it with, and how we manipulate the surface, for instance, by tilting it or shaking it as it dries. If you get the idea that there is a world of opportunity, you're right.

Whatever method and whatever resist is used, one thing is constant: The resist must be completely dry before etching. Resist the urge to move to the next step too quickly… your patience will be repaid.

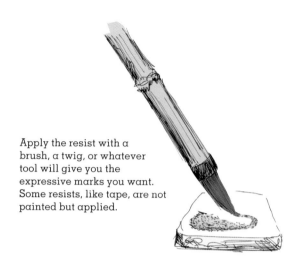

Apply the resist with a brush, a twig, or whatever tool will give you the expressive marks you want. Some resists, like tape, are not painted but applied.

It is also possible to apply resist with a rubber stamp, either commercial or one you make yourself.

For the construction of this piece, it made sense to assemble the box first, then water etch. After etching, I used Syringe PMC to create another level in the decorative pattern. The shallow etch is enhanced with a liver of sulfur patina.

Buddha in a Box
Fine silver, sterling, Nepalese handmade chain, white heart and chevron trade beads.
1" by 1½" by ³/₈"

ETCHING WITH WATER

Because PMC is water soluble, a damp sponge is all that is needed to remove those areas that are exposed. When I first started using this process I recommended an elephant ear sponge, a soft natural sponge available at craft and ceramic supply stores. With that too I work near a shallow dish of water, rinsing the sponge frequently as I go. This makes it easy to refresh the water and to catch the PMC slip that is being wiped away. Recently I have switched to a moist towelette (a.k.a. wet wipe). The wet wipe is already the perfectly wetness.

Make the sponge wet, then wring out most of the water (or use the wet wipe). Rub this across the PMC surface and you'll see that a small amount of metal clay comes away on the sponge. The pressure, angle, and direction of the rubbing stroke will de-

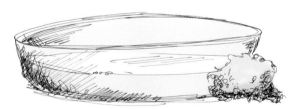

The tools needed for water etching are simple—water and a sponge. A shallow dish is easiest to use, but any container will work.

pend on the nature of the pattern, and offers a little control. Imagine a pattern of parallel lines. Rubbing in the direction of the lines will quickly etch deep troughs between them, creating furrows like a plowed field. Rubbing across the lines will remove less material and probably leave the ridges crisper. Soft materials (like the sponge) will reach into small areas, where cloth will leave a gentler, more rounded relief because it does not reach into every cranny.

As the process continues, dip the sponge or towelette into the dish to clean it, wring it out , and repeat. The material that is being removed will end up in the bottom of the dish, where it can be recovered, either as slip or, with a little effort, as reusable clay. Stop when the clay body becomes spongy or soup-like. Let the piece air dry before continuing.

It can be tricky to know when to stop etching because the resist makes it difficult to see exactly how deep the etch has gone. Use magnification to inspect the etched surface closely to be sure you have achieved your goal. It is frustrating to remove the resist only to discover that you wish you'd gone a bit deeper.

When the etching process is complete, set the PMC aside to dry in preparation for firing. As before, this can be simply air drying, or you can use heat or dehydration. Note that some of the resists melt at low enough temperatures that they might start to burn away during drying. This is not a problem, but

might explain that odor you smell.

Fire at any of the firing schedules for PMC+. I fire at 1650°F for at least ten minutes. Many surface finishes look great on a water etched piece. I often use a wire brush with soap and water to get a satin finish, then hand-burnish the high areas (the areas that were covered with the resist) to bring them to a bright shine. This finish, glossy on the high areas, satin finish on the low areas, enhances the low relief texture.

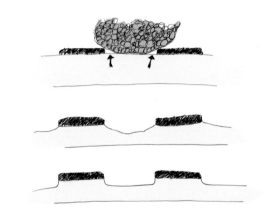

You can control the character of the etch by the type of sponge, the direction of the wipe, and how many passes you make. The spaces at the arrows in the first image show how a light wipe avoids touching the areas close to the resist. A quick, soft wipe will give the rounded contour of the middle image. To get sharper definition, scrub in all directions, and press harder, as in the bottom drawing.

Prismacolor pencils are used in the low areas, which were left in their unpolished, straight-from-the-kiln condition.

Pin #1, Square Pin Series
Fine silver, colored pencils.
1¼" square

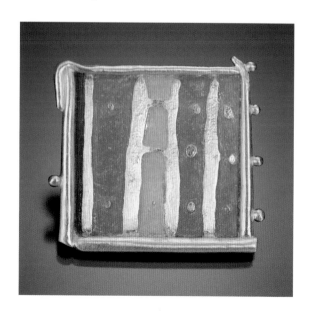

Using etched surfaces

Of course etched surfaces look great all by themselves, but it is worth mentioning at least a few of the many techniques that work well with the controlled relief achieved through etching.

Enamels have been used for centuries, and very often require cells or pockets to hold the glass powders into place. Obviously, water etching is made to order, especially because fine silver is a preferred metal for enameling. The technique called basse-taille uses translucent enamels fused into recesses with patterns on the floor. These are enriched and magnified by a layer of glass. There is no reason why "cold enamels" like resins can't be used in the same way.

Aura 22, a gold layering material that was born in the PMC research laboratory, is another terrific partner for water etching. The recessed areas are ideal candidates for the gold material. Paint it onto the PMC immediately after firing, while the silver surface is uncontaminated by soap, oils, and pollution. Follow the directions on the package to develop a high karat rich gold embellishment.

At the other end of the spectrum, colored pencils can be used to ornament an etched surface too. Wax pencils such as Prismacolor can be used on a matte silver surface. Because they are fragile, they should be used in recessed areas that are protected—in other words, exactly the situation that is created by water etching!

Basse-taille enameling makes excellent use of the water etching technique. Use a translucent enamel to fill a recess that has texture or ornament on the floor.

In a more contemporary process, use the recesses created by water etching to color a design with wax pencils like Prismacolor.

Water etching can stand alone as an interesting surface design, but this pendant has added sparkle with a coat of glitter nail polish

Glitter Square
Fine silver, dichroic glass, glass beads, nail polish. 2" high

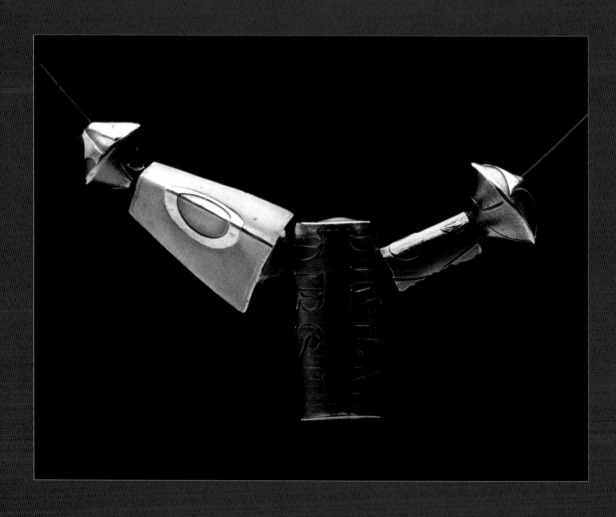

Flying Saucers
Fine silver
center bead: 3" high

J. Fred Woell

Coreless Beads

ne of the first things that appealed to me about PMC was the ability to make beads. Most of my metalwork was done through casting, and while I have enjoyed the complicated steps of making wax models, spruing, investing, and eventually seeing my ideas realized in metal, after having done it a few thousand times, the thrill sort of disappeared. And even for someone who does a lot of casting, making beads that way is tricky.

Then, along came PMC! Because of the microscopic pores between silver particles, the usual concerns about trapping air were no longer relevant. I could form beads around almost anything that burned up, confident that the fumes would simply pass out of the bead before the metal fused solid, leaving, at worst, a bit of ash that needed to be removed from inside the bead during clean up.

Well, maybe it wasn't quite that easy after all. Paper clay, a version of papier maché made with paper flour, sounded like an ideal material, but all commercial versions included other ingredients that left the paper clay hard as a rock. We could use Styrofoam, but this creates an offensive odor, especially when making more than a few beads at a time. As the search for a perfect core material continued, it occurred to me that perhaps there was a way to avoid the core altogether.

BACKGROUND

I was lucky enough to be part of the group of artists gathered at the Haystack Mountain School in the early summer of 1996. I've always been interested in new materials—my graduate work in the 60s was focused on the sculptural use of epoxy resins, which were brand new at the time. I think one of the things that appealed to me about metal clay was the freedom from conventions and preconceptions. In a field as old as jewelry making, we are always operating in relation to what has come before, either by echoing the voices of others, or by pushing back against what has already been done. In PMC we had a material that had no precedents, no expectations about what could and couldn't be done.

Another thing that appealed to me about PMC was that you don't need a lot of training to start getting results. I taught college level metalsmithing for several decades, and it always struck me that students' ideas were compromised by their lack of technical skills. Sometimes their dedication to mastering technical skills came at the expense of their ability to express themselves. I enjoy teaching PMC because of the freedom it allows. I've been teaching it now about as long as anyone, and I'm still enjoying the discoveries that seem to appear at every workshop.

WIRE ARMATURE

This process strikes a chord with me because it forces a bit of chance and serendipity into the making process. The idea is to make a hollow form that will be closed (or "decked") in the dry-but-unfired state.

The first step is to make an armature from wire. My approach is to take several inches of 12-gauge copper wire (wire commonly used in household wiring) and twist up a variety of shapes that will sit up off the table without rolling out of position when you apply the PMC sheet. Roll out PMC three or more cards thick, then cut out any shape you choose. Any shape will work. I usually use PMC+ but any version of PMC can be used. Drape the PMC shape over the wire in any fashion you desire and set it aside to dry. To speed the drying process, set the assembly on a mug warmer. This is particularly effective because the wire conducts heat and transfers it into the PMC. When the shape has hardened, remove the wire, bending it if necessary to pull it out. Refine the edge with a sanding stick or a knife and make any adjustments necessary to create an appealing bead.

Roll out another sheet of PMC the same thickness and type as the first piece, and be sure it is large enough to cover the open portion. Paint a line of thick slip onto the rim of the dry portion and lay the sheet so it creates a sealed bead. Trim off the excess PMC and set the bead aside to dry. When the joint is firm (don't rush this), trim by sanding or carving with a knife. It is best to drill holes now for the chain or core because it becomes much more difficult to do after firing. Having the holes also provides venting in the firing which is a measure to keep the bead from cracking.

To make a simple and spontaneous armature for a coreless bead, bend up a shape in soft copper wire. Drape a sheet of PMC over this and allow it to dry

Set the piece on a cup warmer or similar heat source. The heat will travel through the wire.

After sanding the edge, paint on a layer of thick slip, then set a sheet of PMC to complete the bead.

CONSTRUCTED VARIATION

Maybe, like me, you'll get excited about the curves and edges and planes that arise spontaneously through this technique, but don't let that enthusiasm make you forget about the PMC construction techniques you already know. Remember that it is possible to build beads from dry components, from textured sheets, and from elements pressed into molds.

REMOVABLE CORES

There are times when we need to work on a core. For one thing, a core allows us to start with a known and repeatable form. Imagine a design that calls for a dozen identical beads, and the difficulties of the wire armature become clear. Also, working on a core provides a solid surface inside the bead, and this is helpful, even necessary, for carving, stonesetting, and some other techniques. But, I wondered, even if we start with a core, do we need to keep it there through the firing process?

Here's a technique I developed that attempts to get the best of both worlds. It allows a core for the first phase of the process, when the bead is being made, but the core is removed before firing,. This avoids the problems of fumes and smell.

The first step is to make a core. In this case, let's assume a core of Styrofoam, and just for convenience, I'll illustrate with a bicone bead. It should be noted, though, that a wide range of core materials and shapes will work well with this technique. One of the advantages of using Styrofoam (besides its low cost and range of hardness) is the fact that it is easy to carve. Spheres are sold in craft shops, but if you want something else, carve Styrofoam with a craft knife and file or sand it to achieve the final form. I like to use foam insulation (usually either blue or pink; sold at lumber stores), but floral or packing foam will also work. Work over a wastebasket, and cut-carve-file-sand to make the core you want. Bear in mind that you are making the inside of the bead, so work smaller than you want the final result to be.

To facilitate handling and to assist in lining up the parts, press a small rod through

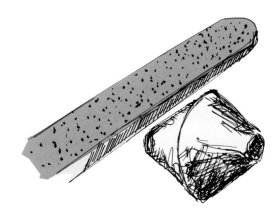

Make a removable core from any convenient material. I like to use dense Styrofoam, but other options include papier maché, polymer clay, and cork clay.

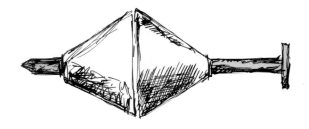

Slide a nail, skewer, or similar rod through the bead. In addition to making a handle for working, this will help align the parts.

the center of the bead. I often use a nail, but a bamboo skewer or other similar tools will do. The next step is to coat the Styrofoam with a layer of wax. This will stiffen the core and provide a surface that adheres better to the PMC layer that comes next. I melt wax in a small container (like a tunafish can) either in a double boiler on a hot plate or on a coffee mug warmer. The latter is very easy, but requires at least a half hour to come to temperature, so plan ahead. You can speed this up by setting a tent of aluminum foil over the can and warmer. Once the wax is molten, it is an easy task to dip the core into the wax and rotate it to achieve an even coating. Allow the first layer to harden (usually only a minute or two), then redip to thicken the wax. Continue until you have a wax layer that is two millimeters thick.

Cover the bead with PMC in any way that is convenient. I usually roll out a sheet and cut this into pieces that I place onto the bead, but it is also possible to paint several layers of slip, allowing each to dry between applications. When the base layer of the bead has been established, ornament the

Dip the core into melted wax. This layer helps the metal clay stick to the core, and also provides an easy release in the next step.

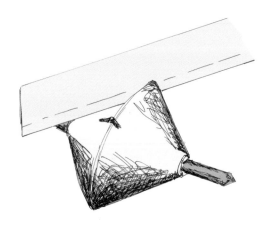

Use a tissue blade or similar sharp knife to slice the core in half, all the way through to the rod. Make a registration mark with a permanent marker to facilitate lining up the parts later.

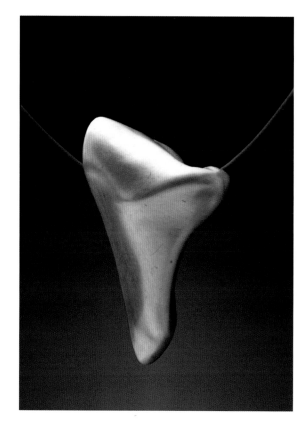

Smooth Tang
Fine silver
1¾" by ⅞" by ¾"

surface in any of the many ways made possible in metal clay. You can layer pieces onto the bead, carve into it, paint on textures, or combine several techniques. And of course, unlike conventional metalsmithing, it is quite easy to undo an embellishment if it isn't working. Complete the bead and set it aside to dry, typically by poking the stick into a block of Styrofoam or a lump of clay that will hold the bead free of contact as it dries.

Examine the bead to determine the ideal equator line, and, if you want to, lightly scratch this line with a needle. Use a razor blade or tissue blade to cut through the damp PMC along this line, to but not through the core material. Make registration marks across the cut with a Sharpie—one mark on one side; two marks on the other. This will make it easier to align the halves later

Allow the PMC to dry completely; overnight is best. Next, using the cut line as a guide, cut all the way through the core until both halves are separated. Gently slide both halves off the rod and sent them onto a mug warmer as shown. Because the PMC is metal,

Separate the parts and set them onto a mug warmer or similar heating platform. This will not only dry the PMC, but it will melt the wax, which allows the PMC parts to drop off the core.

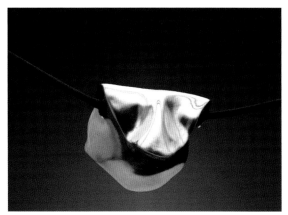

Bye/Fold
Fine silver
1" by 1" by ¾"

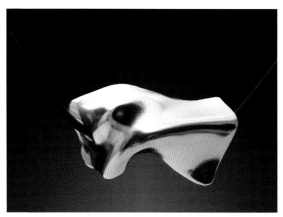

Making Waves
Fine silver
¾" by 1¾" by ½"

if the edges of the bead halves are in contact with the warmer, the heat is transmitted quickly along the walls of the bead. This melts the wax and allows the core halves to drop out easily.

Paint a bead of thick slip onto the edges of the two parts and press them together. I slide the parts onto the nail during this step, using the original holes to assist in aligning the parts. Wipe off any excess slip and set the bead aside to dry. Fire and finish as usual.

Paint a layer of thick slip on the edges of both parts and press them together to dry. In some cases it is helpful to reinsert the rod to align the parts.

Grey Beach Stone
Fine silver, found stone
1¼" by 4 ³/₈" by ¾"

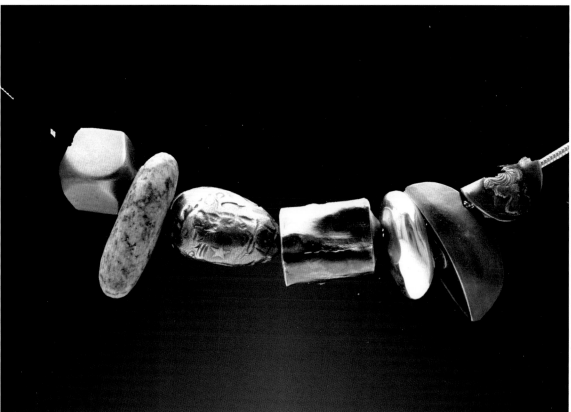